D0971539

WRITING

GETTING INTO PRINT

WRITING

GETTING INTO PRINT

*A BUSINESS GUIDE
FOR WRITERS*

Jo Frohbieter-Mueller

Glenbridge Publishing Ltd.

Copyright © 1994 by Jo Frohbieter-Mueller

All rights reserved. Except for brief quotations in critical articles or reviews, this book or parts thereof must not be reproduced in any form without permission in writing from the publisher. For further information contact Glenbridge Publishing Ltd., 6010 W. Jewell Ave., Lakewood, CO 80232

Library of Congress Catalog Card Number: LC 93-79254

International Standard Book Number: 0-944435-23-8

Printed in the U. S. A.

To my children,
Janet and D. Tom

CONTENTS

Part III

GETTING BOOKS PUBLISHED

Part IV

STRATEGIES FOR SUCCESS

INTRODUCTION

This book is a marketing and business guide for writers. It will teach you how to turn your dreams into reality. You will learn how to sell what you write and develop a writing business. This book will direct you through the process of generating ideas, creating marketable products, identifying appropriate buyers, and making sales of manuscripts to publishers of both periodicals and books. It describes the process of combining writing skills with marketing expertise for maximum effectiveness and profitability.

As you read this book, you will discover that getting manuscripts published is not a procedure shrouded in mystery and dependent upon luck but a process based on implementing a straightforward marketing plan. You will learn to approach the writing and selling of your work as a business venture, using methodologies similar to those used by others to promote their business careers.

Scattered across this land, sequestered behind aging typewriters and high tech word processors, sit writers with stories to tell and ideas to develop. Only a small percentage of these writers will ever see their work in print, discover the pleasure of communicating via the printed word, and experience the joy of being paid for their effort in money, respect, influence, and recognition. The rest will struggle for awhile, trying to figure out how to move from being a writer to a published author, and by the time they finally put away their unpublished manuscripts, the manuscripts will be tattered and the writers worn.

There is a reason some writers succeed while others fail. Writers whose works are frequently published have learned what it takes to make a sale. They know how to target a market, strive to fulfill the needs of editors, and aggressively solicit publishers. On the other hand, many unpublished writers keep writing only what they want, whether or not a market exists for their work, and most of them are baffled by the marketing process.

Writing: Getting Into Print is divided into four parts. Part I includes a discussion of your relationship with the publishing world and an explanation of what it takes to make a living by writing. You will learn what sells best, how to identify marketable subjects, and how to write for your readers. Basic writing tools are discussed along with research techniques used by writers. You will also learn ways to make your work stand apart from the rest of the manuscripts that pour into editorial offices and how to cultivate professional work habits that will enable you to produce a significant quantity of work.

Part II deals with selling articles, short stories, and poetry to magazine publishers. The methods used to regularly find editors interested in your work are explained. Topics covered include how to use marketing references, the mechanics of submitting queries and manuscripts to editors, and how to resell magazine articles over and over again.

Finding publishers for book manuscripts is discussed in Part III. Since nonfiction is sold differently than fiction, the marketing techniques for each are dealt with separately. Besides basic submission procedures, topics include when to use an agent, how to find an agent, how to sell your manuscripts without an agent, negotiating a contract, and after-publication promotion.

Part IV is devoted to strategies for success and ways to turn your writing into a moneymaking business. Included among the topics are the advantages of organizing your writing career as a business rather than operating it as a hobby, tips on creating a professional image, how to take advantage of tax breaks available to writers, and how to manage your time and energy and be more productive.

PART I

YOU AND THE
PUBLISHING WORLD

Chapter 1

THE REALITIES OF THE WRITING/PUBLISHING BUSINESS

Writers and publishers depend upon each other for success. Understanding the needs of publishers and their expectations of you as a writer will help you create manuscripts that have a high probability of getting published. The subjects discussed in Part I apply to both book and article manuscripts.

Publishers and "The Profit Motive"

Publishers are entrepreneurs and profit motivates the publishing world. While you might think you are creating great literature or developing a new idea, publishers will look at your work as a way to earn a profit. And the reason is very simple: if publishers don't turn a profit, they don't stay in business. The publishing business is a big gamble because editors and publishers can't predict with certainty what will attract the buying public's attention. Of every ten books published, four lose money, three break even, and only three earn money. The track record for magazines is just about as bad. Thus, it is not surprising that editors scrutinize submissions with one hand resting on a crystal ball while using the other to thumb through manuscripts.

But you might say, "I'm not interested in money. I just want my work published—to see it in print." Even though money is not your motivation for writing, it *is* the publisher's motivation for printing a manuscript, and you should keep this in mind as you pursue your writing career. It is necessary to produce work that not only satisfies your artistic and intellectual needs but also the needs of potential publishers who want to attract a large number of buyers and readers.

The notion of writing to earn a profit makes many writers uneasy, and some feel they are prostituting their talent in pursuit of the almighty dollar. Many of these writers remain unpublished and unread because of their inability to write with an eye focused on "the bottom line." Perhaps you feel that if a writer is good enough, readers will follow. The problem is, writers who are insensitive to publishers' needs often have trouble getting past the submissions editor, and, for this reason, the best writers aren't necessarily the ones who find publishers willing to publish their work. But, to be fair, it must be added that some editors, many of whom are closet writers themselves, are looking for the manuscript that has both the potential to make a profit and also the promise of being great literature or of being deftly crafted nonfiction.

Word Processors Have Changed the Freelancer's Market

The freelancer's market has changed dramatically in the last decade as word processors have become popular writing tools. There was a sense of euphoria as writers learned to master this new technology. The labor of writing and editing was replaced by computer programs that allowed writers to spend their time grappling with ideas and words instead of "whiteout" and carbon paper. The ease of using a word processor has made writing a leading cottage industry, and editorial offices are being glutted with manuscripts. As a result, it has become increasingly difficult for novice freelancers to sell their material; the output is simply greater than the need.

Word processors have changed the freelance market in several ways. They are influencing both the *quality* and the *quantity* of written work. Better manuscripts are being produced because it is easier to edit works in progress, resulting in compositions that have gone through a continuous editing process. The problem is, word processors have attracted people who have mastered the keystrokes and the technique of putting words on paper but have failed to master the craft of writing. With the help of word processors, untrained and poor writers are producing professional-looking, but poorly-crafted manuscripts, and editors must sift through the bad to find the good. The only way to learn if a piece is worth printing is to read it—and that takes time. In fact, it takes *too much* time to sift through the ever-growing slush pile in search of the few publishable pieces. To avoid reading so many useless articles, magazine editors are depending less on the occasional talented freelancer and the pieces that arrive "over the transom." Instead, they are using more staff-written material and turning to regular contributors to fill their basic needs.

The widespread use of word processors is also affecting the process of finding publishers for book manuscripts. In an effort to cope with the word glut, book editors are relying more on literary agents to intercept and eliminate unsuitable material. Many of the larger publishers no longer accept proposals from authors but depend solely on agents for new manuscripts.

Another mixed blessing of the computer age is the printer that cranks out copies on demand. Unlike the copies of old that were made on copy machines or with carbon paper, printer-generated copies look like originals, and editors have no way of knowing whether they have received a copy or the original unless they are informed by the author. Since copies can be made effortlessly, writers are simultaneously submitting their work to many editors. It's understandable why freelancers use the simultaneous submissions procedure—it allows their work to be seen by more editors and increases the chance for a sale—but the practice takes advantage of editors who spend valuable time reading and evaluating a manuscript, only to learn it has been sold and is no longer available.

As a result of the widespread use of word processors and printers, competition among writers has increased, and only business-wise freelancers can regularly sell their work and get into print.

What it Takes to Earn a Living in This Business

Some of you may be interested in getting a piece published now and then, or maybe you intend to write only a single article or book that has grown out of your work or hobby. Money isn't your prime objective. Others of you intend to be in the *business* of writing and hope to earn a living by selling enough manuscripts to support yourself. If this is your goal, it is important to push a few numbers around so you understand what is required to make this happen.

The price paid for a magazine article varies and is based on the length and quality of the piece, and the circulation, quality, and price of the magazine in which it is published. The publisher also takes into account the background, expertise, and public image of the author before making an offer. The amount paid ranges from nothing (or possibly free copies of the magazine) to $1500 for a full-length piece. Occasionally, an article will bring more, especially if the name recognition of the author or the subject matter will significantly increase sales of the publication. Most magazines pay between $100 and $400 for an article ranging from 700 to 1500 words in length. The beginning and less experienced writer can expect the lower amount, let's say $125 for a piece, while a writer with more experience can regularly bring in $300 to $400 for a brief article. More is paid for longer articles in magazines having a larger circulation. For the purpose of calculating income, let's figure you earn an average of $200 per article. To earn just $10,000 annually, you would need to write and sell 50 articles, or approximately one article each week of the year. An experienced writer can easily write 50 articles per year, but selling them can be a greater task. Even if you accomplish this, you can expect to earn only $10,000. This is not what you would call earning a living.

Can you do any better writing books? It depends. On trade paperback books you can expect to earn a royalty of at least 6 percent of the list price for the first 10,000 to 20,000 copies sold; the royalty usually increases to 7.5 percent thereafter. If a book sells for $10, you will earn 60 cents per book. If 10,000 books are sold, you will earn a little more than $6000, but if 100,000 books are sold, you would make nearly $70,000 (because of the increased royalty when larger numbers of books are sold). Clearly, a lot of books need to be sold to make a significant amount of money. Very few people can make a living writing books.

Still, there *is* a surprisingly simple way to earn a living in this business, but it has never been discussed in print before now. It has been said that the best way to sell a book is to write another book. I have found a much more effective way to promote book sales and one that brings a quicker response. It involves writing a book and then writing magazine articles that refer to the book. A magazine article can bring your book to the attention of hundreds of thousands of readers, and, if a reader's interest is sparked by the article, there is a good chance the reader will look up your book and possibly purchase it. I've written promotional articles for each of the books I've had published, and this has resulted in large book sales. The first book I wrote described how to grow and cook mushrooms. It might have sold 15 copies if I was lucky! To publicize the book, I started writing articles about mushrooms and sold 23 different manuscripts about growing and cooking mushrooms that were published in gardening, family, farming, and culinary magazines. These articles were easy to write because the information was taken from my book. Each article mentioned that I was the author of *Growing and Cooking Your Own Mushrooms* (Gardenway) and, as a result, the book sold beyond my publisher's wildest dreams and has gone through seven printings. Writing articles to promote a book works best if the book is nonfiction, and it is especially effective if the book deals with a subject of widespread interest such as health, making money, or is about how to do something (a how-to book).

It's easier to get articles published in magazines after you have written a book because editors are looking for "authorities" to write for them. After you've written a book, it is assumed you're an authority, and editors proudly inform their readers that you are the author of so-and-so book. This plays right into your bank account. Not only will editors pay more for your work, but the publication of an article on the same subject as your book is essentially a free advertisement that dramatically increases book sales, which means you will pick up more royalties.

Book publishers can't buy this kind of publicity no matter how large their advertising budget might be. The circulation of the major magazines runs between 200,000 and 5,000,000. If you have articles published in numerous magazines, the number of readers who will learn of your book can be quite large.

This sets a cycle in motion. When a book publisher sees that you can and will do this type of promotion, you become valuable to them, and this makes finding a publisher for your next book much easier. The publisher of your first book will be more receptive to subsequent proposals, and this will help you negotiate a larger advance and a better contract. If your next book proposal does not include the kind of material your original publisher handles, you can seek another publisher, taking along a track record of active promotion and good sales. This will cause any publisher to sit up and take notice.

As you can see, there *are* ways to get published and earn a profit in the writing business. The previous tip is just one of them. This book is loaded with proven methods that will not only help you market your manuscripts and get your work into print but also help you make a profit.

Chapter 2

DEFINING YOUR WRITING GOALS

You will accomplish more if you define your writing goals and strive to reach them rather than aimlessly wander from project to project, unsure of what you hope to accomplish. Why do you want to write, and what do you want to write about? Where do you want your work published? How much do you hope to write this year, within five or ten years, or in your lifetime? You should give some thought to each of these questions.

What are Your Reasons for Writing?

The three P's account for most of the reasons people choose to write. They are:

- The PLEASURE of writing

- The desire to be PUBLISHED

- The desire to earn a PROFIT

P for Pleasure: The sheer pleasure of sitting at the keyboard and "jamming" is enough to keep some people writing. Working with words and phrases to flesh out ideas is a "high" only writers can experience. That experience is the best part of writing and is the sole reason many people write.

P for Published: While the process of writing is a joy, it is in sharing their written work that most writers find fulfillment. It is often said that writing is a lonely profession but nothing could be further from the truth. Writing is a way of communicating, and each thought, while formed in isolation, is directed to other people. That is why many writers feel a need—an urgency—to see their work in print; to remain unpublished is to remain mute, unfulfilled, incomplete.

Since you are reading this book you probably feel an urgency to see your work published where others can read and, yes, be *influenced* by it. Writers of articles for major publications can expect to reach many thousands of readers. If it's true that the "pen is mightier than the sword," the number of people who will be motivated by your writing is somewhat daunting, and this will inspire you to try harder to produce work that will enhance their lives and make a positive impact on society.

P for Profit: While you might enjoy writing and seeing your work in print, you probably also expect to earn money from its publication. Actually, you will feel cheated if your work is published but you don't earn a profit because our society recognizes success by paying for it.

Writers sometimes confuse getting paid for their work with earning a profit. Getting paid does not necessarily equate with earning a profit because there are expenses associated with the writing business, and these expenses must be recovered before a profit is realized. While it's true that some publishing houses try to get writers to work for the least amount of money, others pay fairly for the manuscripts they purchase. It is frequently the inexperienced writer who is poorly paid. Those looking for their first or second publication are happy for anything they can get, and some publishers shamefully take advantage of them. But publishers know their livelihood depends on attracting good writers, and most of them willingly pay for quality manuscripts.

Where Do You Want Your Work Published?

You need to think about where you want your work

published before committing words to paper. The number of words printed each year is astronomical, appearing in many forms and in many kinds of publications. Articles are published in newspapers, tabloids, magazines, newsletters, and journals, while books are published in hardback, quality paperback, and mass-market paperback.

If a large readership is your primary goal, then consider writing for magazines because it is through these publications that you can usually reach the largest number of readers. Magazines with the largest circulations reach millions, and many with a medium-size circulation are read by well over 200,000 people. Some large city newspapers also have a sizable circulation, but most of the material they use is either staff-produced or acquired through syndicates.

As you think about where you would like to be published, you might consider that after articles in magazines and newspapers are read, the publications are usually discarded. The articles may immediately impact the readers and influence their opinions and actions, but, with few exceptions, magazine and newspaper articles rarely become a part of the literature that is saved and savored. You are paid a single time for an article published in a periodical, although you can resell it to other publications, which is a rather common practice.

You may prefer to write books. A book-length manuscript allows a writer to delve more deeply into a subject, and authors of published books usually gain more recognition and respect than those who write for newspapers or magazines. Income, in the form of royalties, continues for as long as a book continues to sell, which may range from only a few months to many decades.

Several publishing options are available to authors of book manuscripts. There was a time when most writers wanted to see their work published in hardback because of the prestige associated with that type of publication, but times have changed. Hardcover books cost more to produce than paperbacks; thus the buyers' cost is also increased. Authors and publishers now realize that as the cost of a book goes up, the number of copies sold usually goes down. For this reason, many authors now prefer to have their work published in quality paperbacks where they can attract more readers and at least as much, if not more, income than when they are published in hardback.

There are two kinds of paperbacks. Quality paperbacks are softcover books printed on good quality paper with a format and artwork virtually equal to that found in hardbacks. They are usually distributed like hardcover books and sold directly to bookstores, although some quality paperbacks are now being sold through wholesalers like mass-market paperbacks. Quality paperbacks receive nearly the same recognition as hardbacks. They are reviewed, purchased by libraries, and may be kept on a publisher's backlist for many years.

Mass-market paperbacks are small books, approximately 7 x 4 1/2 inches, printed on poor quality paper, and contain little or no artwork. They are directed to an extremely large audience, and the type of writing found in mass-market paperbacks traditionally includes romance and adventure. The authors of these books are usually required to follow a specific format, sometimes called "formula" writing. However, books on topics of wide-spread interest are also printed as mass-market paperbacks, but many of these were first published as hardbacks. After appearing as mass-market paperbacks, they may remain in print for decades. A good example of such a book is Dr. Spock's book on baby and childcare.

Mass-market paperbacks are distributed to wholesalers who, in turn, sell them to shopping mall bookstores, airport gift shops, grocery stores, and the like. There are over 110,000 potential outlets, besides bookstores, for mass-market paperbacks and, because of their wide distribution, large numbers are sold. Most books published in this format have a brief shelf life—sometimes as short as a couple of months—before being replaced by another title. Much to the chagrin of the authors, reviewers usually ignore mass-market paperbacks, thus they don't get a public airing or receive the attention a review provides. Writers who are published in this format usually gain less prestige, and very few of these books find their way into libraries. For these reasons, many writers are unwilling to write for this market while others have built careers on the spines of mass-market paperbacks.

Just as quality paperbacks are replacing hardcover books, a change is occurring in the role of mass-market paperbacks. Younger readers tend to associate hardbacks with classics and textbooks, but they consider the handy paperback more "user friendly." As a result, the mass-market paperback is becoming a more acceptable format as a younger generation of readers replaces those who grew up on hardbacks. This shift in buyer preference will probably help new or unestablished writers of fiction gain an audience because publishing houses are more willing to take a gamble and print their work, using the mass-market paperback format, since the cost of publishing is much less than publishing a quality paperback or hardback.

Some years ago there were separate hardback publishers and paperback publishers, but now many publishing houses issue both, giving them the flexibility to use the format best suited to a particular manuscript.

Chapter 3

PREPARING FOR A
WRITING CAREER

People who aren't writers tend to think anybody can write—it's just a matter of sitting down and putting words on paper. That certainly isn't the case. While it's true that most people can "put words on paper," only a small percentage of them have the skill to produce compositions that are good enough to be published. Basic writing skills are a necessary prerequisite to getting into print because poorly-crafted manuscripts don't get a second look in editorial offices. You need to know proper grammar, punctuation, and how to organize a composition. You must also know how to hook your readers and how to deliver information in imaginative and interesting ways.

Do You Write Well Enough to be Published?

Be honest with yourself regarding your writing skills. Do you have the ability to produce well-crafted manuscripts and, in the case of nonfiction, do you have the ability to gather and evaluate information and write well-organized, balanced, and thoughtful compositions? If you lack these basic skills, you have two options—either forget about writing or develop the proficiency necessary to be successful.

The best way to master the craft of writing is both to read and write. You must read to see how others write, to learn the cadence of your language, and to gather information. Just as a pianist becomes a better musician by practicing and an artist becomes a better artist by painting, your writing skills will improve, and you will become a better writer by writing. But, unlike a good pianist who can hear a wrong chord when it is struck or a good artist who can see a wrong shape or color as it is applied, you may fail to see the shortcomings of your compositions. Sometimes it's difficult to tell if one's writing is improving. It may be useful to join a writers' group or enroll in a writing class where you will become sensitized to the process of writing, learn how others struggle to improve their craft, and have your work regularly critiqued. It is in this setting that you can begin to evolve into a skilled writer. You should be aware, however, that it takes more than classes and critiquing sessions to become a polished writer; it takes persistence, dedication, and a lot of practice.

Become Proficient With Basic Writing Tools

While you don't need to work with a word processor and printer to be a successful writer, using this technology improves the odds that you will get into print. It will allow you to write more, the work you produce will be "tighter" because of the editing capabilities of word processing programs, and the final product will look professional. Some writers still struggle with typewriters, resisting the move to word processors. More often than not, it is fear that prevents them from investigating and investing in this modern technology, but there is little to fear because the new generation of word processors is designed for the technologically illiterate. These modern writing tools are "user friendly," and it is very easy to learn to use them. If you are a typist, your typing skills can be easily converted into computer keyboard skills.

It's the person who is still pushing a pen or pencil who is out of step with the times. Rarely will a pencil pusher get into print nowadays. It's not that writing by hand precludes writing well; the great writers of the past bear testimony to that. Rather, the time and effort it takes to write a composition by hand and find a typist or keyboarder to put it into an appropriate format puts these writers at a huge disadvantage compared to the writers who use modern technology to help them write, edit, and print their work.

While the quality of word-processing programs used

by writers is important, the quality of the printers used must also be taken into consideration. Printers for word processors include, among others, "dot matrix" in which the shapes of numbers and letters are formed by numerous tiny dots. This type of print is somewhat difficult to read, and many editors refuse to read manuscripts produced by this method. "Daisy wheel" printers produce print that looks like type from typewriters, but the printing process is rather slow. Both "ink jet" and "laser" printers produce excellent quality printing at an amazing speed. If you have a choice, select one of the latter two. They cost a little more than the others but are well worth the extra money.

Another important tool is needed by the nonfiction writer. Keep a good quality camera or two close at hand and learn to take decent photographs. One camera should be loaded with black-and-white film, the other with color film. Photographs accompany articles in most magazines and are used to illustrate some books. Having photos available to supplement a manuscript often makes the difference between making a sale or not. It helps if you take all photos in *both* black-and-white and 35mm color film since some publications want only b/w photos while others use only color. Although you may be writing a piece for a magazine that uses color, you will be prepared to resell it to another that uses black-and-white photos. Or, if you write a book that includes only b/w photos, you will have color photos to use with promotional articles.

Develop Research Skills

Research is an important part of writing, and it takes both good intentions and lots of hard work to become well-informed. You must become conversant in your subject matter and know more than you plan to write if you intend to write convincingly. This will allow you to pick and choose the facts that best meet the needs of your manuscript. Or, as Mark Twain wrote, "Get the facts first, and then you can distort 'em as you please."

Successful writers know how to gather information, whether it's from between the covers of books or personal knowledge acquired through experience and interviews.

Get into the habit of frequenting a library. If you don't know how to use library facilities, either take a class in information retrieval or ask a librarian for help because using a library involves much more than just looking at the books lining the shelves. Modern libraries literally put information at your fingertips, and gathering it may involve you in computer searches, studying microfilms, digging through government publications, or using references that can lead to obscure publications.

Study the literature and make notes as you read. Many writers record information on 3" x 5" cards that can be shuffled as the information is organized. Record anything that might add to the work you are undertaking, whether

it's a single word, a phrase that seems to fit, or deeply con-
voluted ideas.

Keep a record of not only the information you retrieve
from the literature, but also of your own thoughts as your
research develops because some ideas can be fleeting and
lost if they are not recorded. At first new ideas will come
slowly, but they will form more easily as you become
immersed in the subject. It is even useful to keep a notebook at your bedside because, when you are thinking about
a subject during the day, your subconscious can shed new
light on it in the twilight of sleep. These thoughts must be
recorded immediately upon awakening or they will be lost.

Think and work ahead in your research, clipping and
writing down bits of information as you run across them.
While gathering information for one book or article, it is
important to have other subjects gathering momentum. The
offices of most writers are cluttered with notes and articles
clipped from newspapers and magazines. The more organized writers file the clippings and continue to collect them
until a subject seems ripe. This information-gathering
process can go on for years before you are prepared to
write on a subject, but being sensitive to a subject and alert
to facts that can eventually be used will prove to be invaluable when you finally organize the material and start to
write. With this backlog of research already done, it's a
matter of filling in the holes with directed research when
the writing gets under way. During the information-gather-

ing phase you will become aware of publishers who print periodicals or books on subjects that interest you. These publishers may be outlets for your work, so make a list of possible publishers as your research progresses.

Interviewing is also an acquired skill that is invaluable to writers, but it takes practice to learn how to gather and safeguard the information garnered from interviews. Before embarking on an interview, become familiar with the background of the interviewee and have a set of questions prepared. Besides making notes, carry a small, hand-held recorder, and record the interview. As the session progresses, you will need to be flexible and pursue lines of questioning you may not have anticipated but which surface as answers are given in response to your prepared questions.

If you are planning a book, it might be useful to take a class at a community college or even a trip that will give you some basic background, although many successful books have been written by people whose only knowledge of their subject came from the literature and the various media.

Approach the information-gathering phase with commitment and enthusiasm so the research is adequate. You will surely become bored as you investigate certain aspects of a subject, but you must persist with determination and self-discipline; otherwise, you will fail to understand the subject thoroughly and your manuscript will suffer.

Any book you write will include material that has already been published, and it will be necessary to include a review of this information to produce a book that is complete, self-contained, and able to stand on its own. The reader should be able to understand and appreciate your work without having to consult previous publications. Articles include less substantiating material, and the reader is often forced to take a leap of faith and believe the author is making an honest presentation. Of course, the reader may be directed to other sources of information to learn more about a subject. Even if the purpose of your writing is to present a particular idea or theory, an adequate amount of background is necessary to put the idea or theory in perspective. While you should use data that substantiates your position, the composition will be weakened if you do not include alternative points of view.

Even books of fiction require extensive research to create accurate settings, whether they are geographical or historical. Details give manuscripts substance and depth and make them more convincing. Marilyn Durham, the author of several successful novels, rarely sets foot outside her hometown, yet her novels are set in faraway places and made real and believable with facts she gleans from, among other places, the American Guide Series, which is a Federal Writer's Project. This series includes a guide on each of the states and covers basic background, descriptions, history, and details such as the flora and fauna, terrain, and weather conditions. These facts can be easily assimilated into a composition, giving the impression that the author is acquainted with the area and writes from experience. If this particular series is not available in your local library, there is, no doubt, a plethora of other references that would contain this type of information.

Plan, But Not Too Much

If you intend to be a writer, you must write. We all know people who talk about writing but never get to the task of writing because they get caught in the limbo of planning and preparation. Some of these would-be writers take class after class, becoming, in a sense, professional students striving to master the craft of writing. You might need some training but don't let it become a form of procrastination that keeps you from writing. Some of the most successful writers never studied writing but honed their skills with on-the-job training. There are a lot of reasons people fail to write even though that is their goal. They might postpone writing until they gather enough money to buy a typewriter or a computer, or perhaps they overwork their outline before starting to write. Whatever the reason, it's a lame excuse if it interferes with the writing process. To become a published author you must write and submit your work to publishers. It's as simple as that. If a composition doesn't develop the way you had hoped, learn from your mistakes, but carry on, be tenacious, and keep writing.

While too much planning can get in the way of your writing, too little planning can also hamper your career. Plan how to approach a specific project, whether it's an article or a book. This will help you proceed without too much backtracking and save time in the long run. A well-thought-out and detailed outline is one of the easiest ways to plan and organize a subject in preparation for writing a manuscript, and it is well worth the time and effort it takes. Refine the outline as the writing progresses until it reflects what you intend to include in the composition and its order of presentation. If you are working on a book manuscript, the outline can become the Table of Contents. If it is a manuscript for an article, the outline can be used as part of your query letter.

Get into the Habit of Writing

Make discipline a part of your daily life. On many occasions I've been asked, "How in the world do you write a book?" The answer is always the same—"everyday." It doesn't matter how large a task, it must be done a little at a time. In the case of writing, it is done one word or one phrase at a time, and it's always a surprise and a delight to watch a composition develop. A single day's work may not seem very impressive, but after a week the pile of paper starts to grow. In a month it feels good to press the pile between your fingers and feel the thickness, and within a couple of months a box is needed to keep the growing stack of papers orderly.

Norman Mailer described a professional writer as someone who could write on a bad day. You will not get much written if you write only when the mood hits. Get into the *habit* of writing and, once that habit is established, the mood will hit at the time you have programmed yourself to produce. It's like eating and sleeping. We are programmed to be hungry at breakfast, lunch, and dinner, and we are programmed to be sleepy at night. You can also program yourself to write at a specific time each day.

Decide how many hours you want to write each day and put these hours on your schedule. Maybe you have only one or two hours each day to devote to writing, but be very hard-nosed about letting another activity pre-empt this time. If you MUST do something else during your writing period, recover those lost moments the same day, or they will be lost forever. Whether you write two hours or eight hours, it's the *regularity* of writing that adds up to paragraphs, then pages, and finally volumes of written material. If you write a single page, or about 300 words every day, you will finish the year with 109,500 words. Thus, a single page, written daily, will yield a full-length book in a year.

You need to write more than one or two hours each day if you intend to earn a living by writing. Just as people pursuing other occupations work at their jobs for eight hours each day, you should expect to spend at least eight hours concentrating on your work. Besides writing, part of your workday will be spent researching material and marketing your manuscripts, and, when you are involved with a major project, it may be necessary to write more than the allotted eight hours to meet a deadline.

Many full-time writers set a goal to write a minimum of 1000 words each day. This is a reasonable goal and one that can be easily reached. Sometimes it's hard to work through a difficult passage, but by forcing those 1000 words, at least something is on paper (or in the computer), and this gives the writer something to work with. Much more can be written on days when the words come easily and the writing is going well.

Keep mum about work in progress. It's hard to keep a new writing project under wraps because it's on your mind practically all the time, but talking about work in progress tends to dissipate the energy needed to bring it to fruition and can jeopardize the entire project. Of course, the subject may have been discussed many times prior to being used as a topic for writing, and during these conversations your thoughts no doubt evolved and became grist for the writing mill. But once the writing starts, "mum's the word"—with one exception. While it's unwise to talk with casual friends and family about your current project, it can be helpful to talk about it with a confidant who can act as a sounding board and help you think and work through problem areas. You are indeed fortunate if you have a confidant who can and will function in this capacity.

Edit Mercilessly

Someone once said to a group of aspiring writers, "Nobody likes to write, but everybody likes to have written." The truth is, writing is hard work. Much care and attention must be given to the mechanics of writing, and it takes a lot of editing to turn an idea into a well-crafted composition ready for publication. Fortunately, the stages of development of our compositions are hidden from our readers who would probably be shocked at our early drafts.

Strive to edit with a cool and discerning eye. Besides catching the obvious errors in grammar and punctuation, slash redundancy and be alert for inappropriate style, pomposity, or clichés that might have crept into your work. Look at the ideas you develop critically, deleting excess verbiage and demanding that logic prevail. Be sensitive to the "weight" given to the various elements within a composition, and make sure it is distributed properly.

Don't finish a project before it has matured. This often happens when a writer is anxious to get into print. It's wise to let a manuscript age awhile before sending it to a publisher because usually you will find things you want to change after the ink is dry, and you have a chance to see your written words from a fresh perspective.

After you have completed a manuscript and edited it closely, ask a friend or colleague to look it over before submitting it to an editor. Select someone who has the background—someone who won't worry about offending you and whose opinion you respect. You will probably be surprised at the errors found, but it is always better for a friend to catch the errors rather than an editor who is considering the piece for publication. A carefully edited manuscript will get a good reception in editorial offices and has a much better chance of getting into print than one that has not had the benefit of close and attentive editing.

Build a Healthy Ego

There is a lot of fear and apprehension among writers. You must believe in yourself if you expect others to believe in you. A healthy ego will go a long way in helping you write well and make you come across to editors as capable, competent, and confident. Many who are yet to be published aren't sure they can really "pull it off" or that their work can compete in the marketplace. Reading another writer's work, while thinking about how your own might fit into a publication, can be a humbling experience, but it's worth remembering that published material has been researched, rewritten, and has gone through a long editing process before getting into print. The best way to overcome being intimidated by the skill of published writers is to read something you have written, closely edited, and have ready to be reviewed by an editor. You will be amazed at how smart the writer is—or appears to be!

Self-confidence also helps in *marketing* your work because an editor can tell by the style of your presentation if you expect your work to measure up to other published material or if you are unsure of your abilities. Even though you must believe in yourself, exercise restraint when presenting credentials to an editor. Don't overstate your background and ability because overt bragging is as damaging to one's image as self-deprecation.

Chapter 4

WRITE TO SELL

If you plan to sell what you write, you must write what will sell; in other words, you must write for the market. You will have a greater chance of *frequently* getting into print if you follow these guidelines as you develop your writing career.

1. Write nonfiction rather than fiction.
2. Survey the market and concentrate on marketable subjects.
3. Identify your readers and define your market.
4. Limit the scope of your subjects.
5. Write positive books and articles.
6. Use enticing titles.

Nonfiction, Fiction, or Poetry—What Sells Best?

Write nonfiction for publication; write fiction and poetry for fun. Write nonfiction if you want to increase the chance of selling your work because nine times more nonfiction is printed than fiction. You may conclude that if you write fiction, your chance of making a sale is about 1/9th the chance of those who write nonfiction, but that is not the case. I have spoken at many writers' conferences and always ask the participants if they write fiction or nonfiction. Invariably, about twice as many people indicate they write fiction as those who write nonfiction. If the same holds true for the rest of the writing community, then those writing fiction aren't fighting a 1 to 9 ratio but about a 1 to 18 ratio. On that basis alone, it only makes sense to write nonfiction if your goal is to sell your work and regularly get into print.

Writing nonfiction used to be considered less of a challenge than writing fiction, depending less on creative skills and more on sheer doggedness, but now writers of nonfiction are gaining more respect. William Zinsser, in the third edition of his book *On Writing Well*, describes nonfiction as "The New American Literature" and argues that "much of the best and most valuable writing of the day is being done in nonfiction."

Subjects available to writers of nonfiction are as varied as the styles and genre available to writers of fiction, with

each appealing to a specific market. Nonfiction can range
from philosophical pieces devoid of hard data but based on
opinions, values, and experiences, to information-packed
manuscripts or how-to pieces. Of these, how-to manuscripts remain the easiest to get into print.

Most writers of nonfiction tend to concentrate on writing article and book manuscripts, ignoring a more lucrative
niche in the nonfiction market, and that is writing columns.
There are several advantages to writing columns rather than
articles. Each new article requires a new "sell," which means
significant effort must be expended in the marketing
process. Sometimes it actually takes more time to sell an
article than to write it. In contrast, *columns* are sold before
they are written, and a columnist may write columns that
appear in each issue of a publication for many years. Thus,
the columnist can concentrate on the business of writing
rather than marketing. A columnist under contract knows
how much needs to be written and when each column is due.

Columnists are selected by two methods. Sometimes
the job is solicited by the writer who sends sample columns
to editors. These samples may have been published in a
hometown newspaper, an in-house business newsletter, a
church bulletin—or they may be unpublished material.
Other times, editors contact writers whose work they have
noticed. A writer who has had numerous articles published
and maybe has written one or two nonfiction books is considered an authority and a prime columnist candidate.

When a writer is contracted to produce columns, guidelines are usually defined that include the general subject, the length of each column, and how frequently they are to be submitted.

Writing columns that appear in print regularly is perhaps the best way a writer can bring in a steady income, but the amount paid will depend on the type of publication in which it appears. Columns printed in newspapers are frequently syndicated, meaning they run simultaneously in many papers. Each paper usually pays very little per column. The price is based on both the circulation of the newspaper and the name and reputation of the writer. Even though each newspaper pays little for a column, the amount earned by the writer can be quite significant if the column is carried in numerous papers. A syndicated columnist is usually represented by a syndication agency that finds new outlets, distributes the columns, and collects fees. Of course, the agency charges a percentage of the money received for these services. The largest newspaper syndicates include King Features, United, Universal Press Syndicate, Los Angeles Times, Creators Syndicates, and Chronicle Features. To learn what these syndicates need and how to submit manuscripts to them, see *The Guide to Newspaper Syndication* (page 260). Other publications listed in the references (page 257) include the names and addresses of most of the newspapers published in the United States. This is valuable information if you want to self-syndicate a column.

Another possibility is writing for your local paper. You'll not be paid much for a newspaper column, but writing for a local publication will allow you to get your views before your friends and neighbors and, as your columns catch on, you will become somewhat of a celebrity in your home community.

Most newspapers with large circulations hire columnists to write exclusively for them. These writers are paid a regular, but seldom a large salary, although their salaries usually increase as they develop a following of readers.

Columns that appear in magazines are usually written specifically for the periodicals in which they appear; i.e., they are not syndicated and the columnist is rarely represented by a literary agency. Publishers pay a premium for this type of material—usually more than for regular articles. Since columns appear on a regular basis and without any marketing effort on the part of the writer after a contract has been procured, this is considered to be one of the best writing assignments.

Perhaps you have no interest in the lucrative nonfiction market and are interested in writing only fiction or poetry. Fiction writers have numerous options and outlets for their work. Fiction includes a wide range of genre but some types of fiction are easier to place than others. There is a big market for juveniles, adventure, and romance in both magazines and books, but the competition makes getting published an exercise in patience even when your manuscripts cover these popular subjects. Still, you can improve your chances of getting published by following the same guidelines that apply to nonfiction, that is, by accurately targeting your readers and tapping into their interests, needs, and concerns.

Are you one of the many writers who dreams of writing "The Great American Novel"? It's tough getting a first novel published, but, as you will learn in Parts II and III, there are marketing procedures that will help you get into print. If you are determined to write fiction and believe you have the talent to succeed, go ahead; just be aware of the odds you are facing.

Poets also have difficulty finding publishers for their work. Books of poetry, even inexpensive paperback editions, rarely recover the cost of printing because, while many people say they like poetry, few are willing to purchase these books. For this reason, publishers shy away from publishing a new talent. Poets should recognize the truth and acknowledge that they are writing for personal pleasure and certainly not to make a profit or even for public recognition. It is the rare poet who gets into print, and rarer still for a poet to see a monetary reward for his or her work.

Poetry contests have become commonplace, and many

thousands of poets enter them annually. Some of these contests are legitimate and strive to recognize talented poets, but others are scams sponsored by publishers with the intention of creating a market for their books. Many of these contests declare every entrant a winner and offer to publish their poetry in an anthology where thousands of other poems appear in tiny print. The publishers are capitalizing on the facts that, (1) few commercial publishers print poetry, and (2) poets are anxious to see their work in print. The price of these books typically ranges from $30 to $60. If each poet, whose work appears in the collection, purchases at least one book (there may be several thousand poets published in each volume), this alone will bring a profit to the publisher. There is nothing illegal in this type of arrangement, but it may mislead writers into believing they are talented and inspire them to continue writing and buying collections of work of questionable quality, produced by struggling poets, rather than that produced by poets who are published because they are talented.

Poets are vulnerable to these contests because most don't realize that there are literally thousands of small magazines and journals in which poetry is printed. They overlook these smaller publications as they try to get published in well-known publications, which is a very difficult task. The key to getting poetry published is becoming familiar with the poet's market and pursuing it with commitment and dedication. (See directories on page 258.)

Greeting cards provide another opportunity for poets. Approximately sixty greeting card companies in the United States purchase verse from free-lance poets. These companies are listed in the *Writer's Market* and in the trade magazine, *Greetings*. If you want to write for this market, become familiar with the lines produced by the various greeting card companies by visiting card racks. Write to the companies that seem most appropriate for your work to learn submission requirements.

Poets can also use their poetry as messages in greeting cards and letters directed to their families and friends. Since poets often write about personal subjects, they can receive much pleasure through sharing their work with these special people.

Poets have other outlets for their work. They have established their own network and organizations where their work can be heard and occasionally published in their club's newsletter. Poets' organizations can be found in most medium-to large-sized communities, and their purpose is to encourage each other and provide a forum for sharing their work. Many of these organizations promote contests, bestow acceptance, and grant awards to their membership. If you are interested in joining this type of group, watch the newspaper for poetry readings or contact colleges, universities, and arts councils in your area to learn about the organizations and when they meet.

*Survey the Market and Concentrate
on Marketable Subjects*

With so many periodicals and books in print, it's practically impossible to find a subject that has not been covered. The trick is to write about old subjects in new ways.

The question of what to write about is one that persist-
ently troubles many would-be writers. Some years ago,
Wendell Johnson wrote an article entitled, "You Can't
Write Writing." He explained that there is no such thing as
writing in the abstract—you have to write about something. I'm frequently approached by people who tell me
they want to be writers and are seeking advice. Of course,
the first question I ask is, "What do you want to write
about?" I'm always startled to learn that many of these
people don't have a subject in mind. Few of these people
will be able to develop writing careers because successful
writers have stories to tell, ideas to promote, and things to
teach, and they frequently find there aren't enough hours in
a day to get all of the words on paper.

The best subjects are those that come naturally. Perhaps your professional life has provided you with special
knowledge that would be of interest to others. Maybe you
have amassed facts and skills through your hobbies and are
anxious to share your discoveries. These might be excellent topics to develop and write about, but if you intend to
produce manuscripts *continuously* and *regularly,* you must

reach beyond your hobbies and work experiences to identify subjects. Finding marketable subjects is a matter of watching, listening, reading, and participating in a variety of activities. Being involved with your subject matter will make your writing fun and easy, and when you write about subjects drawn from personal experiences, your work will have a ring of truth and credibility. On the other hand, your writing will be less convincing if you must gather all of the information you use from other sources. To work with a subject that is foreign to you, one that requires you to dig for every shred of information, can make your working hours miserable. Still, even though you are familiar with a subject, extensive research is needed to fill in the gaps in your knowledge if you intend to write a well-rounded manuscript.

Although a subject may interest you, it may not interest an editor. Editors are very sensitive to their readership and are looking for material that will pique readers' interest, satisfy a curiosity, enhance lives, teach something—or, in short, persuade the reader to buy a book or magazine. As a writer, you need to anticipate the interests of both readers and editors.

One of the best ways to get a feel for the market and identify the kinds of subjects that attract publishers is to regularly browse the bookstores. It is here that you will pick up trends and learn what the various publishers are printing. Finger the books and flip through a few to get a feel for quantity, quality, and illustrations. Which subjects get the best location on the shelves? Notice which publishers are well-represented and which publishers print books on subjects that interest you. These might be the ones you will pursue when you have a manuscript to sell. Watch the customers. You can learn about what people are looking for in books by watching how they react to them in bookstores. Can you see why customers pick up one book over another? A clever title or an attractive cover may be enough to induce customers to take a closer look. How do they handle the books? Do they turn the pages and stop to read a line or two, or do they study the chapter headings in the Table of Contents? Do these potential buyers look at the illustrations, or do they study the cover? What is it that makes the customer either return a book to the shelf or take it to the check-out counter? Keep these observations in mind because they can influence the kinds of manuscripts you produce and affect whether your writing attracts publishers and readers.

While browsing in bookstores, take a moment to study the periodicals. You can pick up valuable information from these magazines. A brief glance at a magazine will give you a feel for the style, format, and content. Some are breezy and superficial; others are solid and filled with information. Some are obviously not the kind you could write for, but others will immediately feel right for your work.

Writers' references, such as *Writer's Market,* list the editors' names and addresses for many, but not all, of the magazines published in this country. Some are not listed because they use only staff-written material, but others not listed might use freelancers' work. Editors for publications that are not included in writer's references could be receptive outlets for your manuscripts since fewer writers will submit material to them. You'll find where and to whom to submit manuscripts on the first or second page of each magazine.

As you search for marketable subjects, whether for book-length manuscripts or manuscripts for periodicals, you need to be alert to trends or new movements and become knowledgeable about them before they become commonplace. Make every effort to learn as much as possible about emerging subjects, and determine if you would like to write about them. I have done this very successfully throughout my writing career. Several years ago I became aware of a renewed interest in stained glass. Books on crafting stained glass panels were starting to appear in publishers' catalogs, and it was just a matter of time before this interest would invade Europe. To take advantage of the growing market, I learned to make stained glass art, wrote a how-to book on crafting with stained glass, and promptly sought a European publisher. The book was purchased by a British publisher who printed it in English and in several foreign language translations. I used the same approach when it became apparent that home businesses were becoming popular. Nearly twenty million people are running businesses from their homes, and many more are trying to figure out how to get one started. That's a huge market that could be easily targeted. To learn a home business from the inside, I started and operated one for several years, and I now have several columns that appear monthly in magazines, scores of articles in print, and a couple of books published on the subject of getting a home business "up and running." The experience of actually operating a business made writing the books and the many articles and columns very easy.

One has but to look around to recognize the multitude of subjects close at hand; it's just a matter of identifying them. For instance, if you garden, you toil in fertile soil because editors are always looking for gardening articles. Grow something out of the ordinary, record it on film, and use your experience to write an article. Include recipes if the plants produce food; if the plants yield flowers for bouquets, include a photo of an arrangement. The recipes and photos will help sell the article.

Another good way to find subjects is by studying newspapers, especially the lifestyles sections. The stories in newspapers are often about local happenings, but they can be applied to a wider audience. Also, a newspaper article will provide a framework on which to hang an article, and the story will give you leads to help you delve deeper into the subject.

You can make more money writing about subjects that have an ongoing interest rather than those of interest for a limited time. For instance, an article featuring an interview with a foreign ambassador on an American cruise might sell shortly after the cruise, but an article about why cruises are becoming an increasingly popular way to vacation can, with a little rewriting, be sold many times to different periodicals.

Publishers have little interest in publishing personal memoirs, but they receive more unsolicited manuscripts of this type than any other. The reason people like to write memoirs, besides being a topic close at hand, is they require little research, and, if the information is partly fabricated, who will know (or care)? With few exceptions, memoirs are unpublishable because, other than the immediate family, most people won't buy a book about your life and thoughts. Of course, memoirs of the rich and famous are of interest and are marketable.

Take into account your background and intellectual capacity as you consider various topics. You will learn quickly that although a topic might be appealing, you may lack the background to grasp the complexities of it and to research it adequately, therefore making it difficult to produce a well-balanced manuscript.

Whether you write political essays or celebrity interviews, short stories or scholarly treatises, each requires an appropriate writing style and a set of linguistic and intellectual tools that will give substance to the material. Before telling your friends and colleagues that you are writing this wonderful manuscript, and before soliciting a publisher, it's a good idea to make a detailed outline and take a hard, honest look at the project in order to decide if you can successfully complete it. Do you have the capacity and skill to research the subject adequately and commit the ideas and information to paper? After carefully evaluating a proposed project, you may realize that the work can't be accomplished or that, to get it done, you will need to commit more time and energy than you are willing to give. It can be very embarrassing and can damage your reputation if you announce prematurely that you intend to write about so-and-so, only to discover that you are unable to produce the manuscript. This type of failure can even damage your self-confidence, which must remain intact if you are to be an effective and persuasive writer. So don't take on more than you can accomplish, and make every effort to complete those projects you DO undertake.

Limit the scope of your manuscripts. If the subject you select is too broad, it may be impossible to cover it in a reasonable manner in a brief (1000-2000 word) article. Also, it is difficult to find a publisher for a book that is too broad in scope. This is because the target market is difficult to define, and it's next to impossible to distill a broad subject into a promotional one-liner, thus the book would be difficult to promote. When contemplating a topic, define exactly which aspect of the subject you will cover. Rather than writing about mental illness, for example, concentrate on a specific mental disorder; rather than writing about premarital sex, maybe something about safe sex on college campuses would be more salable; or, instead of hot *meals* for cold days, make the piece more specific and write about hot *soups* for cold days. Each of these examples concentrates on a limited part of a larger subject, and this is exactly what is needed to attract an editor's attention.

As you consider various subjects, keep in mind that positive writing sells manuscripts. Negative subjects encounter stiff opposition in editorial offices, and they rarely get into print even if they explore legitimate problems. Of course, many articles and books have been written about adversity, but the ones that get into print usually discuss ways to overcome misfortune and this makes the material of value to readers.

Identify Your Readers and Define Your Market

You will increase your chances of getting into print if you target a specific group of people and write for them. You should take into account your readers' age, vocabulary, background, interests, and needs.

"Narrowcasting," or directing a publication to a defined and limited segment of the market, is a trend that has become common in recent years. It has proven to be a windfall for freelancers who write for magazines because, with a few changes that direct a manuscript to a specific market, an article can be published in several different magazines whose circulations don't overlap. Thus, through narrowcasting, an article can be sold many times with only minor rewriting. Consider, for example, the huge number of people who read religious magazines. Dozens of religious publications serve these people, but, since they rarely read the publications of religions other than their own, an article can be published in several magazines without being seen by the same readers. Religious magazines not only target different religions, but they also target different age groups and different sexes within the religions. There are Catholic publications directed to adults and others are directed to children. Some are written specifically for Catholic females and others are written for aging Catholics. This same specialization holds true for the publications of other religions. Some editors of religious publications want the articles they print to include Bible verses and to have an obvious religious orientation, while others seek only a subtle reference to religion, preferring to show the effect of religion through the behavior of the characters or the development of the story. As you can see, it is important to know the style and orientation of a magazine before attempting to write for it. By the way, religious magazines are notoriously poor paying, some paying as little as 1 or 2 cents per word. Still, many writers are more interested in getting their work read and their ideas aired than being adequately paid, and editors of religious magazines always seem to have a backlog of manuscripts on file from which they can pull material to fill their publications. It's relatively difficult to get printed in religious magazines because of the stiff competition from other writers, many of whom are preachers who are trying to earn a little money by converting their sermons into manuscripts.

Writing regional material is another way to define your readers and your market. Magazine articles are rather easy to place in regional publications (see page 73). On the other hand, a *book* directed to a regional market would not appeal to most publishers because of its limited sales potential, although a few publishers specialize in printing books with a regional appeal.

While many book publishers direct their publications to very defined markets, others look for manuscripts that will attract a wider audience and generate more sales. Why write a book for a regional audience when, with a little extra effort, you can cater to a much wider market? When possible, write with national and international sales in mind by using a local subject as an example of a more widespread phenomenon. Writers often dismiss or fail to realize the potential of international sales. A book about how a town solved water pollution problems could interest readers in New York as well as in London or Sydney. Instead of a title like *Stopping Water Pollution in the Ohio Valley,* the title could be *Solutions Used to Halt Water Pollution.* A few international examples are usually all that are needed to make a book acceptable to this wider market. When writing for an international market, avoid slang, locations, or monetary terms that might not be understandable to foreign readers.

Textbooks can also be written to appeal to a wider readership. They are sometimes written, not only for academic use, but also as trade books, and this significantly increases the number of potential buyers. When this is done, it is important to be sensitive to the nonacademic reader and make the book more accessible by using endnotes rather than footnotes. Other techniques for making specialty books more appealing to nonspecialists include placing technical information in tables or appendices where they can be skipped over, if desired, and designing the headings and format with the nonspecialist in mind. If this is done carefully, it will not detract from the technical point of view but can increase the appeal of the material to nonspecialists. An author who hopes to appeal to both the academic and trade market must not assume the reader is familiar with previous works on the same subject. When referring to other publications, instead of writing, "According to Berstein"—and assuming the reader is familiar with the source—write, "According to Roberta Berstein in her book *The Constancy of Change . . . .*" This enables the less informed reader the opportunity to find the source, if desired.

The Importance of Enticing, Descriptive Titles

It is helpful to select a "working title" when you start writing a new manuscript, and refine the title as your work progresses. By the time you submit the manuscript to an editor, the title will have evolved into the best you can produce. A title that clearly identifies the work is important because, with the avalanche of new books published each year, it is difficult to remember oblique titles, but a title that clearly defines a work is remembered. There is another reason for selecting a descriptive title. It is much easier to write advertising copy for a book with a good title than for one that needs explaining. If the subject of the book cannot be conveyed in a brief title, you might use a short main title with a more descriptive subtitle. The title might influence where a book is listed in catalogs and how it is categorized in bookstores and libraries. The business book *Swimming With the Sharks* was sometimes listed among biology books rather than business books, and as a result, many potential buyers were unaware of it. It's worth mentioning that a descriptive title makes a book easier to find through computerized card catalog searches.

Just as book manuscripts with positive titles sell better than those with negative titles, article manuscripts with positive titles also have a much easier ride through editorial offices. I remember a piece I did about engaged couples spending a disproportionate amount of time preparing for their thirty-minute wedding but giving only fleeting attention to the years of married life that followed. The article was titled, "Are You Spending Too Much Time and Money Preparing for Your Wedding?" The article was sent to several periodicals but didn't sell. When the title was changed to "Prepare for Marriage While Making Wedding Plans," it sold immediately even though the body of the article was exactly the same. The importance of titles became very clear to a professor at a local university. He taught biology and offered a class called "How to Care for House Plants." The class was cancelled because few students enrolled. The next semester he offered the same class but named it "Plant Parenthood" and the class was filled to capacity. I've noticed the importance of titles many times as I've worked as a literary agent trying to sell writers' manuscripts. There is no doubt that the ones with good titles have a better chance of getting into print.

If you feel that the title you propose will enhance the sale of your book, and to change it would jeopardize the book's success, then it is necessary to include the title as a part of the book contract. The contract should include a clause stating the title of the book and that it cannot be changed without your permission. Still, it's worth remembering that editors and publishers also want large sales, and when they suggest a title change, the purpose is to attract a wider readership. With their experience in trying different titles and seeing the resulting sales, it may be wise to consider their proposals carefully, and try to understand why the title they suggest will enhance sales.

PART II

GETTING ARTICLES, SHORT FICTION, AND POETRY PUBLISHED

Chapter 5

PLANNING YOUR
MARKETING STRATEGY

Getting Articles Published

Most writers enter the freelance writing business by writing magazine articles. This allows them to get a feel for what is required to produce publishable material before spending months or years preparing book manuscripts. Literary agents rarely handle nonfiction articles or short fiction because they cannot make a large enough profit selling to periodicals; so, if you write articles or short stories for magazines, it's up to you to sell them.

Fortunately for freelancers, the magazine industry is alive and well. While the number of books purchased is declining, the number of magazines being printed is increasing. According to Samir Husni, a professor at the University of Mississippi and an authority on the magazine industry, there are 65,000 periodicals published each year in the United States alone, and the average life span of new magazines is around 3.7 years, or more than twice as long as it was ten years ago. Some, perhaps many, of these periodicals would be right for your work. In spite of the plethora of magazines in print, most writers who are just entering the freelance business have trouble finding outlets for their work. Without a knowledge of the periodical industry, they are attracted to publishers with whom there is little chance of selling their manuscripts, and they are sometimes dismayed at the difficulty encountered when they present their precious jewels to editors. Many quickly discover that writing an article is the easy part; selling it takes another set of skills. It's not uncommon for full-time freelancers to spend as much as a fourth to a third of their workday in pursuit of sales because they need to keep numerous articles in press if they are to earn a steady income. But successful freelancers DO find outlets for their work and you can too.

Your Marketing Strategy

Your marketing strategy should begin before a single word is written. Even though a host of writers are competing for the same space, editors must regularly fill their publications, and you will be viewed as a valuable contributor if you can supply articles they can use.

The key to getting published and building a successful freelance career is learning to match your work with the right publications at the right time. *The main reason article manuscripts are rejected by editors is because the subject matter is not appropriate for the publications to which they are submitted.* Therefore, you are positioning your work for acceptance or rejection when you choose subject matter. Selecting subjects was discussed briefly in Part I, but, since this is such an integral part of succeeding as a freelancer, the process of subject selection, as it applies to periodicals, will now be explored more thoroughly.

Subject Categories

Subjects that can be explored in articles can be divided into four basic categories. The first category includes current events such as political turmoil, celebrity interviews, epidemics, or new fads. Writers who work with these subjects must find publishers quickly, before the public interest wanes and editors move on to other happenings. Current event articles don't have a long "shelf life" and usually can't be resold like articles written on subjects in the remaining categories.

The second category includes subjects of ongoing interest such as childcare, education, travel, religion, hobbies, history, nature and the environment, relationships, home and garden, health, and business. Interest in these subjects continues from generation to generation, and articles addressing these topics can be resold, with a little updating, for many years. Also, as our population ages, there is a growing need for articles directed to senior citizens.

The third category includes the enormous number of "how to" articles; some of these overlap with the previous category. This type of article has proven to be a windfall for freelancers because writing "how to" articles is very straightforward, they are relatively easy to sell, and they can be resold many times. These articles might inform readers how to prepare a sack lunch, build a solar home, master a computer, earn income, grow a garden, craft an item, or care for a pet, among a world of other topics.

Holiday material makes up the fourth category. A writer can keep busy writing nothing but holiday articles— how to decorate, gifts to give, who to entertain, what to serve, the history of a holiday, new twists to an old celebration, and on and on. Holidays are dispersed throughout the year and writing about them can be a full-time career. Since most editors select articles six to nine months in advance of publication, holiday writers must be aware of article scheduling and submit their queries and manuscripts at the appropriate time (see page 89). This category is overlooked by most writers, but writing and submitting holiday-oriented material is a good way to get published regularly. Also, these types of articles can be recycled year after year.

Select a Topic with Multiple Sales Potential

You will increase the chances of selling your work if you concentrate on subjects that can yield numerous articles that will fit into many different publications. To write a knowledgeable composition you must become an authority, of sorts, and you might as well use the information you have acquired to write several articles. When writing on a very limited topic, one that is appropriate for only one or two magazines, you can run into a problem if neither magazine accepts the piece. You might end up with an article but no outlet, and even if it is published, the chance of reselling the article is limited. It is wiser to select topics that can yield articles of interest to a wide range of magazines and ones about which many articles can be written. Because you will be writing several articles on the same subject, the articles you produce, especially the later ones, will have a mature, seasoned quality because of your familiarity with the subject.

Ask the following questions as you consider topics for magazine articles:

1. Do many periodicals publish this type of material?
2. Can the subject be adapted to both general and specialty magazines?

3. Can several or many articles be written on the topic?
4. Can articles on this topic be adapted to different markets without excessive rewriting?

If you can answer "yes" to each of these questions, chances are the topic is worth investigating and developing into a series of articles.

Kinds of Periodicals

Many types of periodicals use free-lance material. By becoming familiar with the various kinds of outlets, you can plan your marketing strategy, select subjects that are appropriate for multiple periodicals, and adapt an article to a variety of publications.

Consumer Publications

Consumer publications make up the bulk of the free-lancer's best outlets and are directed toward a variety of interests and demographic groups, e.g., hobbyists, a specific sex, age or interest group, although some appeal to a more general readership. Consumer publications are usually nontechnical in nature.

For the past several years, hundreds of new consumer magazines have been started annually, but during this same period, many others have failed and have gone out of print. Still others have changed their name or emphasis, all in an effort to attract a larger number of readers. It is important to track the magazines that might carry your work, not only to make sure that they are still in print, but also to help you adjust your manuscripts to fit their editorial style.

Consumer publications are directed to nonprofessionals and are divided into the following categories. Study these categories as you consider possible topics you might write about.

Animal magazines: These publications cover pets, show animals, racehorses, and wildlife. At least 40 publications. Example: *Horseman Magazine.*

Art and Architecture: Articles about art, art collecting, and architecture. At least 35 publications, most of which contain an abundance of photographs. Example: *Art Times.*

Associations: This category encompasses club magazines of national organizations such as Kiwanis, Scouts, or The Toastmasters. Contributors are usually associated with the organization in whose publication their work appears. Over 150 publications. Example: *Kiwanis.*

Astrology, Metaphysics, and New Age: Articles used in these magazines cover such topics as the occult and faith healing. At least 20 publications. Example: *Astro Signs.*

Automotive and Motorcycle: This group of publications concentrates on maintenance, operation, performance, and vehicle comparison. At least 40 publications. Example: *American Motorcyclist.*

Aviation: This category is directed to professional and private pilots and aviation enthusiasts. At least 15 publications. Example: *Flying.*

Business and Finance: Business news, trends, and ideas to increase business are covered. These periodicals are usually loaded with success stories, but technical pieces are commonly covered in business trade journals. Over 60 publications. Example: *Forbes.*

Business Opportunities: This category is directed to those who are interested in starting a new business. At least 20 publications. Example: *Small Business Opportunities.*

Career, College, and Alumni: Magazines addressed to the students, alumni, and friends of a specific institution are included in this group. There are several hundred publications, but many are only open to freelancers who are students or alumni of the publication's home school. Also included are publications that explore career and job opportunities. Example: *Princeton Alumni Weekly.*

Child Care and Parental Guidance: This category provides information on pregnancy, infancy, child development, and parenting. Over 45 publications. Example: *Growing Parent*.

Contemporary Culture: These periodicals target a young adult audience with articles about politics, gossip, entertainment, and fashion. More than 25 publications. Example: *Quality Living*.

Detective and Crime: Accounts of criminal cases and espionage are the main focus in this group. At least 20 publications. Example: *True Police Cases*.

Disabilities: Some of the magazines in this category only print articles written by disabled people. They are directed to the disabled and to those who care for them. More than 20 publications. Example: *Arthritis Today*.

Entertainment: Home video, TV, dance, theatre, adult entertainment, celebrity interviews, trends, and upcoming productions are discussed in these publications. Over 40 publications. Example: *TV Entertainment*.

Ethnic/Minority: The interests, concerns, and traditions of ethnic, minority, and religious groups are covered in these periodicals and include, among others, Jewish, Hispanic, Afro-American, and Italian interests. Over 50 publications. Example: *Ebony*.

Food and Drink: This category includes articles about

gourmet cooking and the good life. At least 35 publications. Example: *Bon Appetit.*

Games and Puzzles: Puzzles, brain teasers, and computer and video games, among a host of other challenges, are presented in these journals. More than 20 publications. Example: *Dragon.*

General Interest: This category, directed to young and old in all strata of the population, contains articles on a wide range of subjects including world affairs, photo features, travel, life styles, and religion. Over 40 publications. Example: *Reader's Digest.*

Health and Fitness: Health and fitness topics for a general audience are covered in this group. Over 50 publications. Example: *Weight Watchers Magazine.*

History: Articles in these publications rehash past events for history enthusiasts. At least 40 publications. Example: *American Heritage.*

Hobby and Craft: This category is for the hobbyist and collector and covers subjects as diverse as antique collecting and woodworking. More than 50 publications. Examples: *Popular Mechanics* and *Crafts 'N Things.*

Home and Garden: Articles about interior design and gardening make up the bulk of these magazines. Over 40 publications. Example: *Better Homes and Gardens.*

Humor: While many publications include humor, these magazines are filled with one-liners, gags, cartoons, and prose humor. More than 20 publications. Example: *Mad Magazine.*

In-flight: These magazines are given to airline passengers. The diverse subject matter favors visual articles with a large number of photographs. Since subject matter is so diverse, articles that have appeared elsewhere may be appropriate for in-flights. At least 10 publications. Example: *USAir Magazine.*

Juvenile: These periodicals are written for children from 2 to 19 years of age. They cover a wide range of subjects with each magazine directed to a specific age group and emphasizing a different style and content. Over 60 publications. Example: *Boys' Life.*

Literary and Little Magazines: Publications in this category contain fiction, poetry, book reviews, essays, and literary criticism. Some are published by writers' groups and colleges, and many have a scholarly orientation. Most literary magazines have small circulations, and although there are exceptions, a large number of them don't pay their authors except in contributors' copies. There are several thousand literary publications, and many of them are listed in *The International Directory of Little Magazines and Small Presses*, Dustbooks. Example: *American Short Fiction.*

Men's: Directed to men, these magazines contain sex-related topics, celebrity profiles, erotic themes, relationships with women, personal experience, think pieces, and some investigative pieces. At least 30 publications. Examples: *Fling, Esquire, Playboy.*

Military: These publications contain articles directed to military personnel and military families. These magazines review battles and include articles about weapons systems, historical/nostalgic, travel, and pieces of interest to military wives. More than 30 publications. Examples: *Army Magazine* and *Off Duty Magazine.*

Music: Music instruction and performance are the thrust of most music magazines. At least 40 publications. Example: *Bluegrass Unlimited.*

Mystery: Detective and suspense stories, and fictional crime stories are the core of these journals. At least 20 publications. This genre is also included in the literary section. Example: *Alfred Hitchcock's Mystery Magazine.*

Nature, Conservation, and Ecology: Environmental issues, wildlife, nature preserves, and recycling are the main topics covered in this category. More than 40 publications. Examples: *Audubon* and *Sierra.*

Personal Computers: These magazines carry articles on new products, technology, computer games, construction projects, applications, and troubleshooting. At least 20 publications. Examples: *Byte* and *PC Computing*.

Photography: Written for the hobbyist, these publications discuss darkroom equipment and techniques, and all aspects of photography. Includes photo features. At least 15 publications. Example: *Popular Photography*.

Politics and World Affairs: Current events, business, national and international news, and political opinion are covered in these magazines. More than 30 publications. Example: *Mother Jones Magazine*.

Psychology and Self-Improvement: These publications include articles about self-improvement, applied psychology and personality studies, and techniques for effective living. At least 20 publications. General interest and men's and women's magazines also carry this type of material. Example: *Celebrate Life*.

Regionals: These magazines and tabloids are distributed to defined geographical or political areas—a city, county, state, or region. Many writers disregard them, thinking they only appeal to a limited audience, but regionals give writers an opportunity to sell the same article repeatedly because the audience in the different regions does not overlap. A basic article can be customized to appeal to different regions by including just one or two sentences that relate specifically to the region in which it will appear. Hundreds of publications. Example: *Inside Chicago.*

Relationships: These journals are directed to people interested in alternative lifestyles and include articles about gays, lesbians, and singles. Some include pornography; others don't. Opinion sells here, along with general interest with a gay slant, and how culture shapes sexual values. Some use erotic fiction. More than 30 publications. Example: *Changing Men.*

Religious: Spiritual experiences are printed in these publications and most of the material makes some moral or religious point. The articles cover nontechnical discussions of theological, Biblical and ethical topics, social problems, and political issues. Hundreds of publications. Example: *Christianity Today.*

Retirement: Magazines for those over fifty. They contain profiles of senior celebrities and articles about second careers, hobbies, retirement ideas, as well as general interest stories. More than 30 publications. Example: *Mature Lifestyles.*

Romance and Confession: These publications cover all aspects of relationships and include stories about true love and confession, problems and solutions. At least 20 publications. Example: *True Confessions.*

Rural: These magazines concentrate on rural lifestyles and include articles about crafting, farming, environmental issues, gardening, along with general-interest articles directed to the rural family. More than 30 publications. Example: *Farm and Ranch Living.*

Science: These magazines cover science fact, fiction, and fantasy for readers of all ages. They also include non-technical but knowledgeable articles about engineering and technology. Also, stories about new products based on sci-entific knowledge are printed. At least 35 publications. Example: *Popular Science.*

Science Fiction: These magazines print science fiction and personal experiences relating to the occult and psychic; they also print horror stories. More than 40 publications. Example: *Isaac Asimov's Science Fiction Magazine.*

Sports (all kinds): There are magazines printed for every type of sports enthusiast. The subjects covered range from archery to wrestling and include publications focused on baseball, bicycling, boating, bowling, fitness, golf, guns, high school sports, horse racing, hunting and fishing, martial arts, running, snow sports, soccer, tennis, water sports and many others. Several hundred publications. Examples: *Snowmobile Magazine* and *Runner's World.*

Teen and Young Adult: Directed to young people between 13 to 19 years of age, these periodicals deal with teen problems, interview/profiles of well-known singers, actors, sports figures, and contemporary teen issues. More than 40 publications. Examples: *Seventeen* and *Teen Magazine*.

Travel and Camping: Travel tips and stories for tourists and campers telling them where and how to travel is the main focus of these publications. Articles cover resorts, cruises, hiking, camping, historic sites, sports vacations, national and state parks and forests, and personal experience. At least 75 publications. Examples: *AAA Going Places* and *Backpacker.*

Women's: Subjects covered in this category of publications include the changing roles of women, love life, health and fitness, emotions, crafts, community projects, family relationships, and self-improvement. More than 50 publications. Examples: *Cosmopolitan* and *Entrepreneurial Woman.*

Trade and Technical Publications

Trade journals, sometimes called technical, professional or business journals, focus on a particular occupation or industry. There is sometimes confusion over the use of the term "trade journal" because it conflicts with the term "trade book." Trade *journals* are periodicals directed to professionals and business people involved in specific trades while trade *books* are directed to nonprofessionals and cover a wide range of subjects and genre (see glossary). Trade journals include publications directed to people involved in practically every profession and trade, from advertising to veterinary medicine. They contain technical articles written by professionals and practitioners and are designed to help the reader do a better job or understand something about the industry. These publications accept articles from freelancers. In fact, a freelancer can focus on a specific industry and be published regularly in trade journals. Or a freelancer might write articles or columns of general interest for a variety of trade publications. For instance, an authority on tax law might do a regular column for a variety of journals by tailoring tax tips to fit each industry. An article about safety in the work place could certainly be adapted to fit several trade journals. Since trade journal editors receive far fewer submissions than their counterparts at consumer magazines, there is a good chance of making a sale and getting into print when you approach them with proposals.

Trade journals usually carry shorter articles than consumer publications, and the subject matter must be of immediate value to the readers. Since the readers are intelligent, literate, and knowledgeable, it is imperative that the articles be well-researched. Professionals are usually a good source of information because many of them are anxious to talk about their professions and can provide insight into trends and important developments in their industry. Trade journals usually have smaller circulations than consumer magazines, although the amount paid for article manuscripts is about the same, with some publishers paying a pittance and others paying a reasonable amount.

Scholarly Journals

Articles carried in scholarly journals are usually based on original research and written by the scholar or scholars who conducted the research. Prior to acceptance for publication, the articles are evaluated by the author's peers to determine if the manuscript contains new information and if the research procedures used to acquire the knowledge were adequate. Scholarly journals are not outlets for free-lance writers.

Chapter 6

FINDING OUTLETS FOR NONFICTION, SHORT FICTION, AND POETRY

Marketing Directories

The publishing business is always in flux. Some publications are financial failures and go out of print, but there are always new ones getting started. It is important to know the status of the various publications as you plan your submissions. You need to know not only that a particular publication is still in print, but much more. The information that changes most often is the name of the publication's editor. Editors frequently change jobs, and it is advantageous to know the current editor's name so you can address your inquiries and submissions properly. Submissions addressed to "Editor" tend to be read last, or they end up in the slush pile that is picked over by subordinate employees.

There are several indispensable marketing directories that can help you keep up with the changes in the publishing business. These directories are filled with lists of editors and publishers who purchase manuscripts produced by freelancers. Annual directories listing publications that purchase nonfiction articles, short fiction, and poetry are listed in "References" on page 257, along with a list of writer's periodicals. These periodicals are useful because they contain current tips on the types of material specific editors are needing.

Of the several directories available, the *Writer's Market* (Writer's Digest Books) remains the reference used most widely by free-lance writers. Not only does it contain over 4000 outlets for the freelancer's work, but it is updated annually and costs around $25, making it accessible to most writers. Besides *Writer's Market*, the *Novel and Short Story Market (N&SSM)* (Writer's Digest Books, $20), and the *International Directory of Little Magazines and Small Presses (IDLMSP)* (Dustbooks, $25) are invaluable to writers of fiction and poetry. Many of the other directories are quite expensive, some costing hundreds of dollars. Also, the information in the larger publications is not as easily accessible as it is in *Writer's Market, N&SSM,* and *IDLMSP,* where the editors have distilled and presented the information in an easy-to-use format. It's wise to supplement the information you gather from these directories with information from the larger reference works and by reading current issues of writers' magazines. Most libraries own at least some marketing references and writers' periodicals.

Because of the changes constantly occurring in the publishing world, information in writers' reference books quickly becomes obsolete, and it is necessary to purchase a new edition each year if you are a serious freelancer. Depending on the type of material you write, you need either a current issue of *Writer's Market, N&SSM,* or *IDLMSP* sitting on your desk. The problem is, so many writers refer to these references for guidance that large numbers of articles pour into the editorial offices of the publications listed in them. This is particularly true of the publications listed in *Writer's Market* but less so for those listed in *IDLMSP.* One way to beat the competition is to purchase the new edition as soon as it becomes available in late September or early October and immediately send articles or query letters to the *newly-listed* publishers. New listings are identified in *Writer's Market* with double daggers. These are the easiest markets to approach and may result in a sale if a manuscript is sent shortly after the new edition of the directory appears in bookstores. At this time the editors of these publications will have few submissions from freelancers so the chance of making a sale is significantly increased. Sometimes a sale to a new publication, or an old publication that is listed for the first time, will not only result in a sale, but, since there isn't much competition, your work might attract an editor's attention, and you will be asked for more material at a later date.

Evaluating Possible Outlets for Your Work

It is wise to heed publishers' needs as you consider where to place your work. Writers' directories indicate what publishers and editors need. A typical listing in *Writer's Market* contains the following information (other references list some, but not all, of the categories described below while others list still different types of information):

(1) The name of the publication and the name(s), address(es) and telephone number(s) of the editor(s).
The editor's name and address is needed as you prepare your query or cover letter. Although the editor's telephone number is listed, don't call unless you are writing about a current event that needs to get into print quickly. In this case, a telephone call will enable you to learn immediately if the editor is interested in seeing the material.

(2) The percent of articles written by staff and free-lancers.
This number indicates how seriously free-lance material is considered. If a publication is primarily staff-written, the chance of making a sale is greatly reduced.

(3) The frequency of publication.
One factor that influences the number of manuscripts

an editor purchases is the frequency of publication; the more often a publication is printed, the greater the need for material to fill the pages. Thus, your chance of being published in a weekly is about five times greater than being published in a monthly. Editors of weeklies need a huge amount of material, and many of them give serious consideration to the submissions of freelancers. Unfortunately, there aren't many weeklies in print. Regionals that publish Sunday supplements are good outlets for freelancers. Once you are published in a Sunday supplement, the editor may be inclined to look to you for more material. Apparently, few freelancers submit material to them, so the chance of a sale is relatively good.

A few magazines appear only quarterly or biannually, and several, such as *The Old Farmers' Almanac*, are published only once each year. Nonetheless, if you have manuscripts that would be appropriate for these periodicals, there is no reason to ignore the infrequent publications as you consider outlets for your work. I have been published in every type of publication—from dailies to annuals (including *The Old Farmers' Almanac*)—and find this diversity of outlets gives the freelancer a variety of opportunities.

(4) To whom is the publication directed?

This information is important in deciding the syntax, subject matter, and detail to use in an article. While the young, middle-aged and older populations may be interested in the same topic, the subject would be treated differently for each age group. For instance, if you are writing about hearing loss, you might explain to the young how loud music damages eardrums, the middle-aged would be interested in how machinery in the work place causes damage, and the older reader would be curious about how hearing loss can be treated, but each article would use the same basic information.

(5) When the publication was established.
This fact gives you a sense of the permanency of the publication. While you might be less inclined to submit manuscripts to editors of new journals, these may be precisely the editors who are looking for new writers. Yes, it's worth approaching the editors of new publications with queries and manuscripts.

*(6) The **amount** paid for free-lance material and **when** it is paid.*
The amount paid for nonfiction, fiction, and poetry ranges from a couple of free copies of the issue in which the work appears to a hefty sum of money. Some publishers pay by the word, with a range of one cent to one dollar per word, while others pay a fixed amount for a complete article. In the latter case, while the exact word count is not taken, the length surely influences payment. Beginning writers are sometimes so anxious to get into print that the amount received for their manuscripts doesn't seem to matter. That euphoria doesn't last long. Payment becomes an important factor to a writer after the second or third publi-

cation. Most successful writers refuse to be published if they aren't adequately compensated.

When a writer is paid should certainly be considered as you evaluate possible outlets. Ideally, you want a publisher who pays "on acceptance" rather than "on publication." When a publisher has money invested in a manuscript, there is a greater urgency to get the material into print than when none of the publisher's money is at risk. A piece can remain in an editor's files for years if there is no financial commitment. During this time the article can become stale or outdated, and if the editor decides it isn't something that can be used after all, the writer may be left with a worthless article. That rarely happens if the article is paid for "on acceptance."

(7)   The circulation size of the publication.

It is helpful to equate a magazine's circulation to something that can help you visualize that number of readers. *Mother Earth News* published the first article I ever wrote. It has probably published the first article of many, now established, writers because it publishes hundreds of articles yearly, thus the chance of a sale is relatively good. Like many of its writers, I submitted an article to *Mother Earth News* because I read the magazine and felt in tune with the material they published. The circulation of the magazine at that time was 750,000, and the publisher claimed to have over one million readers. I didn't think much about the meaning of those numbers until a few weeks after the sale when I was attending the

Indianapolis 500 race. The mass of humanity overwhelmed me and, when it was announced that nearly
400,000 people were in attendance, I suddenly realized
the meaning behind the circulation size of *Mother Earth
News*. It meant my article would be seen by nearly twice
as many people as the sea of humanity that swelled (and
swilled) around me. Visualizing the huge number of people who read my work has made me try harder to be a
responsible writer. During the early years of my writing
career I never bothered with publications having circulations of less than 50,000, thinking the number of readers
who might see my work wasn't worth my effort. Then,
one evening, while watching the crowd at a basketball
game, I learned the stadium was packed with 12,000 people. As I watched those people, I realized it would be an
honor to write for and be read by this number of people,
and since that time I've written for small as well as large
publications—if they pay a reasonable amount for the
manuscripts they purchase.

On the other hand, the circulation of some publications
is quite small—sometimes less than 100, and you have to
ask yourself if being read by this number of people fits
your goals. It may. When the circulation is very small, the
pay is usually small to nonexistent.

(8) Is a byline given?
You need a byline if you are striving to develop a
name in the writing business. Even if your main purpose
for writing is to earn money, and name recognition isn't

that important to you, always seek a byline because name recognition will lead to higher payments for your work.

(9) Rights purchased.

The rights you sell will affect your income. If you sell "all rights" to a piece of written work, you will not be allowed to sell it again, but the company that purchases it can use it in a variety of publications. A publisher will pay more to acquire all rights rather than limited rights, but you will probably lose money in the long run. Some publishers won't purchase an article unless they can have all rights, so you must decide if it's worth what they offer. If you have been trying to sell a manuscript for a while but have been unable to attract a buyer, it might be wise to unload it and move on to a more profitable project if a publisher who demands all rights becomes interested. It is usually more lucrative to sell "first rights," which means the publisher can publish the piece before anyone else, after which you can sell other rights to other publishers. Definitions of the various kinds of rights are discussed more fully in Chapter 7 (see page 120).

(10) Time between acceptance and publication.

Some publishers plan way ahead, putting their magazines together as much as nine months to a year in advance of publication, while others have an incubation period as short as one to three months. It is important to know the lead time for each magazine, especially if you are proposing a seasonal or holiday story. It takes some planning to get to press on time. Let's say you want to do a story about a Christmas tradition. The December issue comes off the press in November, and the magazine you hope will publish the story purchases all articles six months in advance of publication. That would be May. Therefore, you need to send a query at least nine months in advance (March) in order to give yourself time to write the piece should the editor be interested in your idea. What if the editor isn't interested? By the time you learn the editor has rejected your proposal it may be too late to send it elsewhere. Do you have to wait another year to send out another query letter? When working with seasonal material, it only makes sense to send out several (or many) queries to different editors simultaneously. Inform them it is a simultaneous query. If they are interested in your proposal, this will motivate them to respond quickly. You could grow old waiting for a chance to write the piece if you send a single query for seasonal material. There is another option. If you want to write the article, go ahead and write it, but continue the marketing procedure until you locate a publisher. After the piece is written you should send the complete manuscript to editors who don't insist on queries, and send queries to editors who prefer them.

(11) Preferred type of submission.
Some editors will read only queries while others prefer to see completed manuscripts. What you submit is very important; this is discussed more thoroughly in the next chapter.

(12) The kinds of material needed—nonfiction, fiction, poetry—and the subjects covered.

Read the description of the kinds of materials needed very closely. It's a waste of time, energy, and postage to send a query or a completed manuscript to a publisher if it isn't the sort of material the editor uses. You will not only be wasting your time, but you also will be damaging your reputation and become known as someone who irresponsibly submits material. You certainly don't want to become known as "that nut" who keeps sending in "stuff," regardless of editorial needs.

(13) The desired length of articles, stories, or poems.

The length of articles printed varies among publications. Some print only short pieces with a maximum of 600 words while others prefer 4000 words or more and won't consider anything as short as 600 words. Many publications print articles within a length range, accepting, for instance, pieces running from 800 to 1500 words. Believe the numbers in the listing and don't bother to submit a manuscript that doesn't fit within the guidelines.

The different length of articles used in different publications makes it difficult to resell articles without rewriting—either tightening or expanding them. Fortunately, many publications use articles in the 1000-word range (8 of the 10 listed on page 101 use 1000-word articles). If you are writing a manuscript before it is sold, aim for one thousand words and adjust it, as needed, when the article is sold.

The length of fiction used is also defined in the listings, but a rather wide range of words is often acceptable. The length of the poetry that will be considered for publication is rarely mentioned. Editors are more interested in style— traditional forms, blank verse, free verse or avant-garde— and less interested in length, although most publications are unwilling to consider epics. Generally, more than one poem is submitted at a time, and the listing indicates how many will be reviewed— usually between four and six.

(14) Information about photos that will accompany written material.

Photos sell articles. The chance of selling nonfiction articles is significantly increased if the written work is backed up with good photographs. Some publishers pay extra for photos while others consider them to be a part of the package. Still, if it takes a photo to sell a piece, get into the habit of carrying a camera and document your subject with photos (see page 26). Some editors will use your photos to study the visual possibilities but hire a professional photographer to take the photos that are used in print. This is especially true of the glossy, highly visual magazines such as *Architectural Digest* and *Gourmet*.

(15) The number of articles purchased per issue or year.

This number tells you whether you should bother with a particular publication. Many publications are looking for an occasional gem that comes in "over the transom," but most of their material is staff written. If a listing for one publication indicates that three or four articles are purchased each year, but a listing for another points out that over 300 articles are purchased, there is no doubt where you will have the best chance for a sale. Cross out those that purchase few articles so you don't waste time looking at the listing again.

(16) Tips and other information.

This section usually provides clues that give you some insight into the editor's needs. One editor might note, "If an article needs a bibliography, chances are it's not right for us." In other words, don't go only to the books for information, but gather material from a variety of sources, perhaps interviews or personal experiences. Another tip: "A frequent mistake made by writers is trying to teach too much— not enough entertainment and fun." OK, lighten up! Or, "We assign nearly all of our stories, but, it doesn't hurt for a writer to query with samples and present their idea in a one-page letter." Since the editors say right up front that they probably aren't interested in your work, why waste your time submitting it when other magazines are looking for stories?

Using Your Marketing Reference

As a kid, you were probably taught not to mark in books, but that doesn't apply to your personal copy of your marketing reference. The more notations you make in your marketing directory, the more useful it becomes. There are thousands of listings and it takes close study to find the publishers best suited for your work. You may find yourself repeatedly reading the same listing as you search for outlets. Never read your marketing reference without a pen in hand, and use a pen with ink that won't bleed through to the other side of the page. Circle the important numbers or words as you study a listing. If you intend to write only for larger magazines, circle the circulation size and cross out the listings that are of no interest to you. If you see a publication that might be a suitable outlet for a story that is in the back of your mind, make a notation in the margin of the directory. If you write only for magazines that pay well, circle the pay schedule and cross out those that don't pay enough to warrant your attention. If you are using your marketing reference to best advantage, the listings will be thoroughly covered with comments, slashes, and circles by the end of the year. But an old issue is like a pair of old shoes—you finally get them to fit when they are worn out. I'm always reluctant to replace my old marketing directory with a new edition, because the old one becomes more valuable with each notation. The new issue, however, includes new outlets and corrected information, and it's wise to start all over again with slashes, circles, and comments as soon as the new edition becomes available.

Don't discard the old editions of your marketing directory because they can be of real value. Some publishers ask to bè omitted from the new edition because they are over-loaded with material, but others are deleted because they didn't update their listing or they failed to return it to the editors in time to be included in the new edition. After a couple of years of not being included, the editors of these publications might be receptive to anything that comes their way. Besides sending queries or manuscripts to newly listed publications as soon as the most recent edition is off the press, also send to those that haven't had a descriptive listing for a couple of years. If you are using *Writer's Market*, this is easy to determine because a special section indicates which publications were deleted because they have gone out of print and which were deleted for other reasons. It is easier to sell to publications that are still in print but haven't been listed for a couple of years because the competition isn't so stiff.

Consider the Competition

The competition your work will encounter at the various publishers should be taken into consideration as you select places to submit query letters and manuscripts. You probably already know the competition is tough, but I suspect you don't know what you are actually up against. It might be instructive to take a look at a few publishers and the number of queries and manuscripts they receive.

Editors at *Redbook* acknowledge they receive over 40,000 submissions each year, or over 150 submissions each working day. Only 36 of the 40,000 are printed, which means writers who are sending their manuscripts to *Redbook* have less than a 1 in 1,000 chance of getting their work accepted for publication. There are several reasons so many people are trying to get printed in *Redbook*. In the first place, *Redbook* pays well for the articles they purchase, and secondly, the circulation of the magazine is rather large (3.9 million) so the publication is brought to the attention of many writers. There is a more subtle reason why this magazine receives so many submissions. This publication is read almost exclusively by 25- to 44-year-old women, about half of whom work outside their homes. Many of the other half are at home, sitting in front of their computers—writing, and many of the working women can hardly wait to get home from work so they, too, can get to their computers to write about that jungle out there. These women are writing for *Redbook* because they are familiar with the magazine, and it carries stories that reverberate with the kinds of experiences they have encountered. It just happens that this group of women are among the most prolific of the freelancers who are trying to break into the writing business. They don't realize their time would be better spent writing for magazines whose acceptance rates are more in their favor.

The other large-circulation magazines have as many or more submissions as *Redbook*. Those with the largest circulations attract the most submissions. A couple of periodicals with huge circulations are *Modern Maturity* (over 22 million circulation) and *Reader's Digest* (16.5 million circulation). Editors of these publications receive awesome numbers of manuscripts to be considered for publication. *Reader's Digest* probably has the largest number of submissions because ideas and manuscripts are actively solicited throughout the magazine, and the publisher pays rather well for the material used. On the other hand, *Modern Maturity* is read by retired people, many of whom are trying to start a second career of writing, while others are anxious to share their retirement experiences; thus, the editors of the magazine are inundated with queries and manuscripts. A serious freelancer shouldn't bother sending a query or manuscript to this type of publication because the probability of getting published is practically nil.

Some of the largest weeklies, such as *TIME* and *Newsweek*, are almost entirely staff written, and their editors do not read free-lance submissions. In fact, most slicks (high quality magazines, printed on slick paper and with a large circulation) have a staff that writes the basic material. In the case of women's magazines, this includes cooking, crafts, clothing and make-up articles. Nonetheless, their editors are always looking for the freelancer who can provide an article that is fresh and "off the beaten path" and that can give the magazines a little "heart." The chance of getting published in these types of publications is quite small.

While most freelancers want to be published in magazines with large circulations, the truth is, if they are to be published regularly, it is necessary to rely on magazines with mid-size circulations for most of their sales. There are hundreds of magazines with circulations of less than a million but over 100,000, and still hundreds more with circulations between 50,000 and 100,000. These can be good outlets for your work because fewer freelancers are attracted to them, thus the competition is not so keen, and it is easier to make a sale.

Finding Outlets for Fiction

Most consumer magazines buy and publish nonfiction, but fiction is a little harder to sell. Listed in the table below are a few of the larger magazines that publish fiction and the ratio of stories purchased to the number submitted. As you can see, the numbers are sobering, but the competition varies greatly between publishers.

This type of information can help you make submission decisions based on your goals. For instance, you would be better paid if you sold to *Atlantic Monthly,* but the chance of having your work purchased is very low. Still, being printed in *Atlantic Monthly* holds a lot of prestige. If your goal is to be read by the largest number of people, *Woman's Day*, with a circulation of 6,000,000 and a relatively encouraging purchase/submissions ratio of 1 in 500 might attract you. Of course, if you are looking for a publication with a high purchase/submissions ratio (and a

Name of Magazine	Circulation	Pay	Approximate Ratio of Purchases to Submissions
Good Housekeeping	5,000,000	$1000+	1/1500
Redbook	3,900,000	850+	1/1200
Atlantic Monthly	470,000	2000+	1/1000
McCall's	5,000,000	1200	1/1000
Woman's Day	6,000,000	800+	1/500
Seventeen	1,900,000	600+	1/600
New Yorker	600,000	1000	1/400

better chance to get published), this is the wrong list. Instead, concentrate on the little magazines or regional or specialized markets where the purchase/submissions ratio can run around 1 in 15 or better. The statistics in the following table are typical for publications with smaller circulations; they print a much higher percent of the manuscripts they receive but pay very little for them. Of those listed, the obvious one to try is *Antietam Review* because the purchase to submissions ratio is in your favor and the pay is reasonably good, considering this publication has a small circulation.

Name of Magazine	Circulation	Pay	Approximate Ratio of Purchases to Submissions
Michigan Quarterly Review	2000	$10	1/300
Antietam Review	1500	100	1/50
Indiana Review	600	5	1/100
Pinehurst Journal	150	5	1/15

While *Writer's Market* is the "bible" for writers of nonfiction, *Novel and Short Story Market* and *The International Directory of Little Magazines and Small Presses* (see references, page 257) are the best marketing directories for fiction writers. There are thousands of literary or "little" magazines listed, and many of them receive limited numbers of submissions. Surely, some of these publications would be right for your work.

List the Best Outlets for Your Work

When you turn to *Writer's Market* or another marketing directory, you will probably have a specific story or article you are hoping to place. As you skim through the reference, list each outlet that might be right for the article and make notations about the publications. If your goal is to appear in publications with large circulations that pay well, then indicate the circulation size and the pay schedule of each publisher you include on the list. Also, list the number of words required and any tips that may help you make your manuscript more appropriate for each publication. Finally, rank each publication, with "++++" for the best publishers and a single "+" for less desirable ones. As you prepare a list for one article, you might also make lists of possible publishers for other articles you are planning to write. Make each list on lined paper that can be stored in a three-ring notebook.

The list of possible outlets for a single article, short story, or group of poems might look like Table 1. It would make sense to list these outlets in the order you plan to submit your work, but since you don't know this when you start your search, the "Order of Submissions" is filled in after the list is completed. The list might contain as many as thirty possible outlets.

Let's take another look at Table 1. You might wonder how the order of submissions was determined. According

Make a List of Possible Publishers For Each Article You Write

Table 1

Title of Article: GETTING THE MOST FOR YOUR ADVERTISING DOLLAR

Page in WM	Name of Periodical	Editor's Preference Query/Manuscript	Words Needed	Pay Scale When Paid A/P*	Circulation	Number Purchased	My Rating	Order of Submission	Submission/ Purchase Status
299	Entrepreneur	Query	750-2000	$200-300(A)	325,000	?	+	8	
696	Self-Employed America	Query	150-750	$200-350(A)	300,000	50-60/year	++++	1	
299	Income Opportunities	Manuscript	2000-3000	Good(A)	375,000	45-55/year	+++	4	
666	Working Woman	Manuscript	250-3000	Very Good (A)	950,000	200/year	++++	2	
698	Nations' Business	Query	700-2500	$100-2000(A)	865,000	100/year	+++	3	
297	Business Today	Manuscript	1000-1200	$.15/word(A)	?	40/year	+	9	
701	Small Business Chronicle	Query	750 max.	$5-80 (P)	20,000	?	+	10	
701	Woman in Business	Manuscript	1000-3000	$.15/word(A)	110,000	30/year	++	6	
267	Executive Female	Manuscript	800-1000	$50-400(P)	190,000	60/year	++	7	
268	New Business Opportunities	Manuscript	500-2000	$150-350(A)	200,000	25/year	+++	5	

*(A) = Pays on acceptance
*(P) = Pays on publication

to the notations, *Self-Employed America* pays well for short articles. It would probably be worth sending a query letter to *Self-Employed America* with the hope of making a quick sale. If that query brings a sale, a short article would be written and used as a framework for a more complete article. Since most of the publications listed use articles in the 1000-word range, it would be wise to aim for a 1000-word article. Query letters should be sent to the publications that use 1000-word articles in the order shown on the list. If one publisher doesn't express interest, another one probably will if the proposal accurately targets the publication's readers and is on a topic the editor can't refuse. After the manuscript is completed, and, if the query letters have not attracted a buyer, then the completed manuscript should be sent to those publishers who are willing to read unsolicited manuscripts.

After completing each marketing list, place it in a three-ring notebook. The notebook will become filled with lists for every article you have ever written or intend to write as your writing career develops. It will be explained shortly how these lists will evolve to show when and where queries or manuscripts have been submitted, when and where the manuscripts have been published, and the amount paid for each manuscript.

Chapter 7

SOLICITING PUBLISHERS OF PERIODICALS: WHAT TO SUBMIT AND WHEN TO SUBMIT IT

Query Letters: When, Why, and How to Use Them

Query letters are usually used when trying to sell non-fiction manuscripts to periodical publishers, but it is necessary to send complete manuscripts when fiction or poetry is being marketed.

The purpose of a query letter, from a writer's point of view, is to learn if an editor is interested in seeing and perhaps purchasing the proposed article. From an editor's point of view, the purpose of the query letter is to learn if the proposed article would cover an appropriate subject and if the writer is capable of producing it.

Editors know a query letter is a quick way to separate writers from nonwriters and subjects of interest from those that are inappropriate for their publications. This screening technique is especially useful to them since they often receive a huge amount of mail from anxious writers. For this reason it is important to make your query letter the best you can produce.

Make every effort to make your letter appear as though you are not new to the writing business. Use good quality letterhead stationery that is something other than white so it is noticed and remembered. My stationery is bright pink. An editor might read my query letter, and, after having thought about it, remember, ". . . that pink letter had a good idea." The pink stationery (or any other color) can be easily retrieved from a pile of white papers. Include your telephone number along with your mailing address on the letterhead because editors sometimes call when they see a query letter that interests them.

The format of a query letter is quite specific. It should identify the subject you hope to write about and include a brief synopsis that explains how you intend to develop the subject. Give your qualifications for writing the piece and mention the approximate length of the proposed article. If possible, give the editor the option for a shorter or longer article. You might write, "The article will run approximately 2000 words, but, if you prefer, it can be shortened to 1200 words." Be sure to indicate when you can complete the manuscript. A query letter should be no longer than a single page, so you must make every word count. Match the style of your letter to the style of the magazine in which the article might appear. Writing samples are not required although you might include a few tear sheets, if you have them, or a brief list of published credits and offer to provide writing samples on request.

The editor will make a decision based on your letter. As you become more aware of the ways of the publishing business, you will find yourself spending as much or more time polishing your query letters as the articles that follow. This is time well spent because it will not only improve your chance of a sale, but you can use phrases from the query letter in the article, and the synopsis can be used as a framework for the article.

Don't be intimidated by an editor but lay your goods on the table. The letters of some beginning writers are so wimpy and tentative that they rarely get past the secretary. Remember, editors need good writers, and if you can convince an editor in a single-page query that you can deliver the goods, chances are you'll get the job IF the editor can use an article on the subject you propose. Study the sample query letter that follows:

Use printed letterhead

                                           Date

Ms. Hope M. Daniels, Editor
MILITARY LIFESTYLE
1732 Wisconsin Ave., NW
Washington, DC 20007

Dear Ms. Daniels:

Mushrooms are commonly found on produce
counters, but many young women don't
know how to cook them. I am the author
of _Growing and Cooking Your Own Mush-_
rooms (GardenWay Publishing). I would
like to write an article about how to
prepare mushrooms for MILITARY
LIFESTYLE. The mushrooms discussed in
the article would be the white-capped
Agaricus, the variety normally carried
by produce markets. The article would
run between 1500 to 2000 words, depending upon your needs.

The first part of the article would
briefly discuss the nutritive value of
mushrooms, the different qualities and
ways to prepare the various stages of

mushrooms (buttons, small, large, fully opened), the proper way to wash them, how to use them as a garnish, and storing techniques. The second part would consist of mushroom recipes including, among others, stuffed, pickled, mushroomburgers (to teach kids to enjoy them), sautéed, batter-dipped and deep-fried, and of course, wonderful cream of mushroom soup.

Excellent color slides, showing the mushrooms being used in recipes and as garnishes, are available to illustrate the article.

I will be happy to forward examples of my writing upon your request.

I look forward to hearing from you.

Sincerely,

Jo Frohbieter-Mueller

(*Military Lifestyle* is a publication directed to the wives of military personnel and women in the military. The magazine usually carries at least one article about cooking, and the proposed article was designed to fill this niche.)

A query is not always the best way to approach an editor. While it's true that some editors want to see a query letter before considering a manuscript, others prefer to skip the preliminaries and see the finished product. These editors will review manuscripts that come in "over the transom," as we say in the trade. These are unsolicited manuscripts from unknown writers. Of course, an editor who receives a completed manuscript realizes the author is fishing for a buyer, and the manuscript has probably been on several editors' desks. Consequently, the price offered for a piece that was not written on assignment is usually much less—little more than half of that paid for one written on assignment. On the other hand, a lot of editors rarely enter into a contract on the basis of a query letter, preferring to buy "the bird in hand" rather than risk catching "the bird in the bush," and, for this reason, it's worth covering both fronts by sending queries to editors who prefer them but completed manuscripts to editors who want to see the finished product. Editors' preferences are usually indicated in the marketing directory listings, especially those in *Writer's Market.*

Using the List of Possible Outlets

With a well-written query letter or manuscript in hand, it's time to use the list of possible outlets you have prepared (Table 1). Start sending query letters or copies of the manuscript to editors, following the sequence in the "Order of Submission" column. Only a few submissions are indicated in Table 1, but with an expanded list, you might send out five or six queries or manuscripts at a time. Update the list, as shown in Table 2, each time material is sent to an editor.

As soon as one editor rejects your query or manuscript, check to make sure it doesn't have any glaring errors, and immediately send it to the next outlet on the list, changing it to reflect the needs of that magazine. To wait is to waste valuable time. By listing all possible publishers before starting your search for a publisher, you take the hassle out of identifying another possible outlet each time a proposal is rejected. And since you're following a prearranged schedule of submissions, getting a rejection doesn't carry much of a sting—it doesn't seem to matter that much. Woe is the writer who is bothered by rejection because that is a normal part of the writing business. More is written about rejections later.

When an article is sold, it must be withdrawn from the other editors who have received a copy of the manuscript. By writing letters of withdrawal, you will save the editors valuable reading time, and the editors will realize they are working with a reputable writer whose work is purchased by others. Sending letters of withdrawal is a great way to promote yourself. You can be sure your work will be reviewed with more enthusiasm the next time you submit it. It's smart to follow a withdrawal letter with another query letter or manuscript while your name is still fresh in the editor's mind.

Table 3 shows how the marketing list will look when the article has been sold. The notation at the bottom of the

Use printed letterhead

Date

Ms. Janet McCormick, Editor
AMERICAN BUSINESS
Box 79286
Dallas, TX 75272

Dear Ms. McCormick:

I am writing to withdraw from consideration for publication a manuscript I submitted to you on July 23. The manuscript, titled "Getting the Most for Your Advertising Dollar," has been purchased by another publisher.

Thank you for your consideration.

Sincerely,

Dorothy Johnson

Sample Letter of Withdrawal

Update the List: Keep a Record of Each Submission, Rejection, and Sale

Table 2

Title of Article: GETTING THE MOST FOR YOUR ADVERTISING DOLLAR

Page in WM	Name of Periodical	Editor's Preference Query/Manuscript	Words Needed	Pay Scale When Paid A/P*	Circulation	Number Purchased	My Rating	Order of Submission	Submission/ Purchase Status
299	*Entrepreneur*	Query	750-2000	$200-300(A)	325,000	?	+	8	
X 696	*Self-Employed America*	Query	150-750	$200-350(A)	300,000	50-60/year	++++	1	7/1/93 sent query; Bought, on assign Paid $325
X 299	*Income Opportunities*	Manuscript	2000-3000	Good(A)	375,000	45-55/year	+++	4	9/8/93 sent query; 9/23/93 sent ms
X 696	*Working Woman*	Manuscript	250-3000	Very Good (A)	950,000	200/year	++++	2	7/1/93 sent query
X 696	*Nations' Business*	Query	700-2500	$100-2000(A)	865,000	100/year	+++	3	7/1/93 sent query
297	*Business Today*	Manuscript	1000-1200	$.15/word(A)	?	40/year	+	9	
701	*Small Business Chronicle*	Query	750 max.	$5-80 (P)	20,000	?	+	10	
701	*Woman in Business*	Manuscript	1000-3000	$.15/word(A)	110,000	30/year	++	6	
267	*Executive Female*	Manuscript	800-1000	$50-400(P)	190,000	60/year	++	7	
X 268	*New Business Opportunities*	Manuscript	500-2000	$150-350(A)	200,000	25/year	+++	5	9/2/93 sent query

*(A) = Pays on acceptance
*(P) = Pays on publication

X means query letter or manuscript sent to editor.
Slash through page number indicates editor not interested.

list indicates the manuscript should not be resold for a while. You may think that keeping this kind of record isn't necessary as you try to get your first or second sale, but when you have at least twenty articles in the marketing pipeline, and many in press, you will be unable to remember where you have sent the many queries and manuscripts, and it becomes necessary to rely on this type of chart to keep track of your marketing activities. At this point in your career, it is also necessary to keep a cross-reference so the same editor doesn't receive too many submissions from you within a short time. The cross-reference consists of an alphabetical list of publications to which you submit material, with a notation of each submission you sent and when you sent it to each periodical. Yes, this requires a little bookkeeping, but it is well worth the effort because it allows you to track your submissions and sales accurately.

Responses to Query Letters and Unsolicited Manuscripts

The most common responses to a query or an unsolicited manuscript are, "No, not interested" (rejection), "Yes, would like to see the article on spec" (response to query letter), or, "Yes, can we talk business?" (response to query letter or manuscript).

Rejection

A rejection can mean many things. It can mean that, (1) the editor has already assigned the subject to another

Further Updating Of the Same List

Table 3

Title of Article: GETTING THE MOST FOR YOUR ADVERTISING DOLLAR

Page in WM	Name of Periodical	Editor's Preference Query/Manuscript	Words Needed	Pay Scale When Paid A/P*	Circulation	Number Purchased	My Rating	Order of Submission	Submission/ Purchase Status
299	*Entrepreneur*	Query	750-2000	$200-300(A)	325,000	?	+	8	
X 696	*Self-Employed America*	Query	150-750	$200-350(A)	300,000	50-60/year	++++	1	7/1/93 sent query; Bought, on assign Paid $325
X 299	*Income Opportunities*	Manuscript	2000-3000	Good(A)	375,000	45-55/year	+++	4	9/8/93 sent query; 9/23/93 sent ms; Sold $400
X 696	*Working Woman*	Manuscript	250-3000	Very Good (A)	950,000	200/year	++++	2	7/1/93 sent query
X 698	*Nations' Business*	Query	700-2500	$100-2000(A)	865,000	100/year	+++	3	7/1/93 sent query
297	*Business Today*	Manuscript	1000-1200	$.15/word(A)	?	40/year	+	9	
701	*Small Business Chronicle*	Query	750 max.	$5-80 (P)	20,000	?	+	10	
701	*Woman in Business*	Manuscript	1000-3000	$.15/word(A)	110,000	30/year	++	6	
267	*Executive Female*	Manuscript	800-1000	$50-400(P)	190,000	60/year	++	7	
X 298	*New Business Opportunities*	Manuscript	500-2000	$150-350(A)	200,000	25/year	+++	5	9/2/93 sent query

*(A) = Pays on acceptance
*(P) = Pays on publication

X means query letter or manuscript sent to editor.
Slash through page number indicates editor not interested.

WAIT UNTIL APRIL, 1994 TO REWRITE/RESELL ARTICLE. (With two articles sold, it's a good idea to wait before trying to sell another article on the same subject).
To make sure you remember to recycle this article, make a notation in your daily calendar when new queries should be sent out.

writer, (2) the idea was used in a recent edition, (3) the subject isn't appropriate for the magazine, (4) the subject doesn't fit into the editorial calendar, (5) the editor already has a huge backlog and doesn't need new material, or (6) the query letter or manuscript is poorly crafted and the editor is unwilling to risk assigning or accepting an article based on the lack of skill displayed.

As you can see, only one of the six reasons reflects on the ability of the writer. In most cases, getting an acceptance is just a matter of *matching a story idea with an editor's needs.*

Evaluating your rejection letters can be very instructive. Magazines with small circulations and trade journals receive fewer queries and manuscripts, and their editors frequently send personal rejection letters. They may mention why your proposal or manuscript wasn't accepted, and you can use this information as you rework the material before sending it to another editor.

If you have submitted a query letter or an unqueried manuscript to a large publication, chances are you will get a printed card that says the proposal does not meet its editorial needs. However, if you get a personalized rejection letter, the editor probably thinks your writing has potential and you are worth nurturing. When you receive this type of rejection, it would be advisable to write and ask for an *editorial calendar* for the coming year. With this, you can direct your energies into query letters or manuscripts that will fit upcoming issues, greatly enhancing the chance of having your work accepted. Some editors routinely send editorial calendars to writers from whom they have purchased articles so the writers can see the type of articles needed and plan proposals accordingly. As you study the editorial calendar and consider possible proposals you might prepare, look ahead at least six to nine months because articles may already have been assigned for earlier issues. Send a new proposal based on the editorial calendar to the editor who wrote you a personal rejection letter.

You need tough skin to survive the frequent rejections you will receive in the free-lance business. Some writers become unglued each time a rejection arrives, and you have to wonder why they stay in the business and keep torturing themselves. You will probably collect enough rejection slips to wallpaper a good-sized room, but don't bother to save them or think of what might have been; think instead of what might be.

Writing "On Spec"

Writing "on spec" (on speculation) means the editor is not committed to buying your manuscript but is interested in the subject and wants to see how you write the piece before accepting it. You have to decide if you are interested in this tentative acceptance or if you should move on to the next outlet on your list. It is usually worth accepting the challenge because apparently the subject interests the editor, and the questions in the editor's mind are how well you write and how you will treat the subject. I frequently write on spec because I know I can put together a good manuscript, and if the first editor isn't interested, I can always sell it someplace else. My experience has been that most articles written on spec are accepted for publication.

Query letters are often sent out for articles that have already been written, and, in some cases, they have already been published. These letters are sent in the hope of *reselling* the manuscript to other publications, but the editors to whom you send the queries don't need to know you already have the article in your back pocket. When an editor is interested in seeing an article on spec, and the piece is already written, wait awhile before mailing it to give the impression that you are working on it. In fact, you may be beefing it up or taking fresh photos. (You should take many photos when you first prepare an article so you will have different ones to use each time the article is resold.) Editors are more inclined to accept an article they think you have written in response to their interest rather than one you pull off the shelf. You should realize that reselling articles and making fresh articles from those that have already been published is necessary if you intend to make money in this business. It takes too much time to gather information if it is used only once. When reselling an article, change the title and rewrite the beginning or hook sentence. Use new photos to illustrate the article and provide different sidebars or other auxiliary material and the manuscript will look like a fresh article.

Acceptance

Yes! Thank goodness for sensitive editors who recognize good material when they see it! This is what you have been waiting for, and now it is up to you to negotiate a contract and deliver the goods.

Negotiating a Sale

When an editor expresses interest in your proposal or manuscript, it's time to negotiate a sale. One of the more important financial skills is the ability to negotiate effectively. Most Americans are not adept at bargaining, and they are embarrassed to even attempt it. Yet, this haggling over price is a part of everyday life in many countries. Some people ignore this important part of the publishing game, thinking it has a unsavory stigma attached to it. It doesn't; you should negotiate every sale you make. Negotiation involves deciding what you want, what you are willing to take, and being able to reach an agreement that both the buyer and the seller feel is a good deal. When it comes to selling magazine articles, it's a little difficult to bargain if the article is already written, especially if the price offered is on a contract that arrives in the mail for you to sign and return. That seems so final and it often is. But many articles are sold over the phone when an editor calls and expresses interest in a proposal. The purpose of the call is for the editor to discuss with you the direction of the article and for the two of you to come to a meeting of minds. The price is negotiated during this call. At this point you need to be very sensitive to the meaning of pauses in the conversation and to the game you are playing. If the offered price seems about right, there is no reason to ask for more; but if the offer is too low, you might express dismay and say you are usually paid more for your work and suggest a more suitable price. On the other hand, it may be in your best interest to accept the offer if you feel you could lose the job if you push too hard. However, never give the impression that you are a pushover because you could find yourself writing for almost nothing. Also, if you are perceived as having experience with the writing/publishing business, you have a better chance of not only negotiating a better price, but of getting more writing contracts. You will learn to negotiate with more finesse as your writing career blossoms and you feel more confident of your abilities.

Money is not the only issue to be considered when negotiating the sale of a manuscript. You certainly want a byline and, if possible, the editor's agreement to include a brief paragraph that identifies you. This is usually presented as a sidebar or at the end of the article. If the manuscript is on the same subject as a book you have written, or if it is excerpted from the book, the identification should include the book's title, the publisher, and price. You may also want to discuss writer's expenses if they are out of the ordinary (i.e., travel, long-distance calls, etc.). During this conversation, the editor may offer suggestions and request that specific topics or details be included. A schedule is then set for completion and delivery of the article.

What Rights Should You Sell?

Another issue to negotiate is the question of what rights you will sell. There are several kinds of rights and the main ones are discussed below:

One-time rights: One-time rights allows a publisher the use of your material one time in one publication. This does not guarantee that the buyer will be the first to publish a piece. One-time rights can be sold many times, and this is a good way to increase income from a single article. However, it is unwise to have the same article published in competing publications around the same time.

First rights: These allow a publisher to print an article or story for the first time, but all other rights remain the author's property. Material excerpted from a book *prior to its publication* is also called first rights or first serial rights.

Second or reprint rights: Also called second serial rights, these allow a publisher to reprint an article after it has appeared in another publication. The money paid for second serial rights is usually split between the author and the original publisher. Articles that are reprinted are frequently the result of the second publisher soliciting the original publisher and asking for reprint rights, although sometimes the author or first publisher solicits the second publisher. Second serial rights also refer to excerpts printed from a book *after the book has been published,* and, again, the fee is usually split between the author and the original publisher.

Foreign serial rights: These rights allow a publisher to print material in magazines outside of the U.S.

Simultaneous rights: These are rights sold to several publications whose circulations don't overlap with the understanding that the manuscript may be published in the different publications near the same time.

All rights: When you sell all rights, you forfeit all claims to your work including the right to resell the work to other publications. While editors offer more money to purchase all rights, it is usually in your best interest to avoid this type of contract. However, around 40 percent of trade journals and 30 percent of consumer magazines want to buy all rights, and some of them will not buy a manuscript if they are unable to purchase all rights. In most cases, company policy and the need to ensure an exclusive story makes the question of which rights you sell non-negotiable. You must decide. If the price is acceptable, you may want to sell, but you may be better off rejecting the buyer who demands all rights if you feel you can sell the article several times to other publications. When a publisher purchases all rights, the material can be used in other publications owned by the publisher, or the publisher can resell the rights to other publishers.

Despite these variations, at the time of sale rights may not even be mentioned. The truth is, many publishers don't send a contract and don't discuss rights; they just write in a letter that your article has been accepted for publication and send a check. Legally, you and the publisher are then operating in a grey zone—they don't ask if the piece has been published before and you don't tell them. Perhaps this is not how it should be, but that's how it is.

Writing on Assignment

After agreeing on terms of sale, you are writing "on assignment." This is, of course, in response to a query letter, not a completed manuscript. To reinforce the agreement (which is often arrived at through a telephone conversation), write the editor a brief note expressing thanks for the assignment and reiterating when the article will be completed and the agreed-upon price to be paid for the work. This letter can become valuable if, on completion of the work, less money is offered. Sending a copy of this letter will quickly resolve the problem.

At this point you know you will earn something from the manuscript, even if it is not printed by the publisher with whom you have a contract. There are many reasons an editor may fail to use an article, including inadequate treatment of the subject or failure to address or engage the readers to the editor's satisfaction. Usually it's because of a change in editorial needs. In this case a "kill fee" is paid.

"Kill fee" refers to money paid to a writer if an assigned article cannot be used. Depending on the publisher with whom you have a contract, the "kill fee" can range from 1/5 to 1/2 of the agreed upon price for the manuscript. While it is nice to receive a kill fee for an unused article, an author would rather meet the needs of the editor and be published. After a "kill fee" is paid, first rights to the manuscript can be sold to another publisher.

Cover Letters: When, Why, and How to Use Them

A cover letter is little more than a one or two sentence letter that accompanies a manuscript and says, in essence, "Here it is—the article you agreed to buy" or "an article for you to read and consider for publication"—except you can't make it quite so obvious. The point is, don't say much in the cover letter because the manuscript should speak for itself. Never send a manuscript to an editor without a cover letter.

If the article has been produced on assignment, then the cover letter should mention that the enclosed manuscript, titled so-and-so, has been completed according to the specifications agreed upon at so-and-so time. Little else is needed.

Use printed letterhead
Date

Mr. Walt Sabel, Editor
TODAY'S BUSINESS
2369 Jackson Avenue
Washington, DC., 20069

Dear Mr. Sabel:

Enclosed is the article titled
"Signs: High Visibility at Low Cost"
that we discussed in early July. I
hope the article meets your expectations. If you have any questions,
please don't hesitate to contact me.

I am available for other assignments
and have enclosed my business card
for your records.

Thank you for the assignment.

Sincerely,

Marilyn Henry

A sample cover letter used to accompany an assigned article.

A cover letter accompanying an unsolicited manuscript should be brief, but state why you are qualified to write the piece and perhaps a word about why you sent it to this particular publication.

Use printed letterhead

Date

Ms. Marjorie Pearl, Editor
WOMEN'S CIRCLE
Box 299
Lynnfield, MA 01940-0299

Dear Ms. Pearl:

Please consider the enclosed manuscript for publication in WOMEN'S CIRCLE. "Women are Leading the Way as Home Businesses Make a Comeback" explains why women are turning to home businesses to earn a living.

I operate a home business and am familiar with the advantages and disadvantages of working at or from home. This is a growing phenomenon, and women need to know about this option as they plan their careers.

I have had several articles about
women's issues published in national
magazines; tear sheets are enclosed.
Also enclosed is an SASE to be used
for the return of the photos.

Thank you for your consideration.

Sincerely,

Betty Palmer

(Paper clip a business card to the bottom of the letter with a
notation that reminds the editor of the types of articles you
write. This can result in an assignment at a later time.)

Provide a Complete Package to Your Editor

Strive to make your editor's job easier. Think through
the process of getting an article into print, and this will help
you prepare manuscripts that will meet your editor's needs.

Submit manuscripts on 8 1/2" by 11" white paper.
Don't use light weight, erasable bond; twenty pound paper

containing some cotton fiber is preferred. It is sturdier than paper made from pure wood pulp and holds up better during the editing process.

FORMAT

(Page One)

Author's name   Approximate word count

Address

Phone number

Social security number

CENTER TITLE IN CAPITAL LETTERS ABOUT
ONE-THIRD DOWN THE PAGE

by

Author's name or pen name (pseudonym)

Skip 4 lines.

Indent 5 spaces and start the first paragraph.

Keep margins about 1 to 1 1/4 inches on all sides of the manuscript.

Double space the body of the manuscript.

Don't use a cover sheet.

Don't number the first page. On every page after the first, on the top line place your name in the left-hand corner and the page number in the right-hand corner.

On the final page, after the last line, skip two lines and either type "The End" or "###."

Paper clip pages together (do not staple).

Other tips:

Make your presentation neat, without crossouts or type-overs.

Don't fold a manuscript to fit into a business-size envelope: use either 9" x 12" envelopes, or fold the pages in half and use 7" x 10" envelopes to mail your manuscripts.

NEVER send the only copy of a manuscript or auxiliary material; keep a copy for your files.

Sidebars, Photos, and Illustrations

Most articles published in periodicals have auxiliary

material that reinforces the ideas presented in the text. Auxiliary material includes tables, charts, photographs, line drawings, lists, and a host of other items that are used as sidebars or illustrations. Auxiliary material, along with captions, should be placed at the end of the manuscript. Clearly indicate within the body of the text where each should be inserted.

Many writers do not provide this type of material with their manuscripts, either because they fail to realize the important role it plays in getting manuscripts accepted for publication, or because they feel unskilled at producing it. Even if you are unable to produce professional-quality illustrations and charts, prepare rough drafts to accompany your manuscript. These can be used as guidelines by staff artists. Even when auxiliary material is supplied, the editorial staff of most large, high quality magazines relies on their staff artists to produce the sidebars and photos used to accompany the articles they print.

Nonetheless, there is no doubt but that the writer who can supply a total package to an editor has a much better chance of having work accepted for publication than one who has only a manuscript to offer. This is especially true when approaching editors of small to mid-size periodicals. It's expensive and time consuming for an editor to chase after auxiliary material, and it's understandable why these editors, who usually work with small staffs, are more receptive to manuscripts that don't require this extra effort.

When submitting artwork and photographs, send only *copies,* keeping the originals in your files. You may be required to provide the original artwork to the buyer after the work is purchased, but always ask for the artwork to be returned so you can resell the manuscript at a later date.

As mentioned earlier, photographs are an important part of the total package for articles that appear in periodicals. Unless the listing in the marketing directory states that a specific type of photo is used in the publication, provide both black and white glossy prints and 35mm color slides. Ask for their return after the article is published.

Chapter 8

THE MECHANICS OF SUBMITTING MANUSCRIPTS TO PERIODICALS

When mailing manuscripts, the goal is to have them arrive at their destinations in good condition. While you want your work to stand out from the rest of the manuscripts arriving at editorial offices, you don't want the method of submission to be noticeable. Just slip the manuscript, auxiliary material, and a cover letter into an envelope and send it on its way.

Some publishers prefer to receive submissions on computer disks. This preference is indicated in their listing in marketing directories. Still others are prepared to receive submissions, especially assignments, via modem. This is surely the fastest way to send information, but prior to using this method, it is necessary to contact the publisher to make sure your computer systems are compatible. Most publishers discourage sending manuscripts and queries by fax, although this may be the wave of the future.

A hard copy, or printed sheets of paper, is still the normal method of submitting written material, and that is the method explained here. You will need a few supplies as you prepare to get your manuscripts off to publishers. As mentioned earlier, it's worth the cost of having printed letterhead stationery to convey a professional image. You will need a supply of different size envelopes. The most useful, other than business size, are 7" x 10" and 9" x 12" envelopes. The smaller envelopes are handy for three or four page manuscripts (fold them across the middle), and the larger size is needed for thicker and bulkier manuscripts. A small postal scale is handy because it will allow you to weigh each package, and you won't need to run to the post office each time you prepare a mailing. Be sure to apply adequate postage stamps because you certainly don't want a manuscript to arrive at its destination with "postage due." Purchase a supply of different denomination stamps because most of your mailings will probably weigh more than one ounce and you will need stamps that satisfy the required postage. Keep apprised of changes in the postage rate. Postage to mail the first ounce costs more than additional ounces. Also, when large envelopes are used, and the package weighs one ounce or less, additional postage is required. Call the postal service to learn how much additional postage is needed.

Everything that goes out of your office should have your name and return address on it. Because of the numerous times you will apply this information (to identify artwork, photos, return envelopes, and so forth), you might want to have your name and address embossed on a rubber stamp.

Use clear plastic sheets, with pockets, to present slides and photographs. These allow the editor a clear view of the illustrations and help to prevent damage or loss. Do not write on the back of photos. Instead, print your name and address on a card and slip it into a plastic pocket along with the photographs. Plastic sheets can be purchased at office supply and photography stores.

The customary advice is to send a self-addressed stamped envelope (SASE) with each query letter or manuscript so the material can be returned to you. Or, the editor to whom you have sent your query or manuscript can use the SASE to send a response without incurring the expense of the supplies and postage needed to respond.

What do you want back? You certainly won't submit a dog-eared manuscript to another editor, so, even if the manuscript is returned, you will discard it and make a new copy for the next submission. What if an editor is inter-

ested in the proposal or manuscript? I've learned that
when editors are interested in a proposal or manuscript,
they rarely use the SASE provided, using instead their
company letterhead and envelopes. If they aren't interested, the SASE is used to send you a rejection slip, but
you can conclude that the proposal was rejected if you
don't hear from an editor in a month or two. I tested my
observation that SASEs don't seem to make much difference in the rate of response when I prepared a huge mailing in an effort to syndicate a column. I mailed over 300
proposals; half of the letters contained an SASE while the
other half did not contain one. The response between the
two groups was virtually identical and confirmed my
observation that it is useless to waste money on SASEs. I
believe the value and necessity of SASEs sent with article
manuscripts and proposals has been overstated, although,
as you will learn in Part III, just the opposite is true for
book proposals. Still, what if it *does* make a difference and
you miss a job because you fail to enclose an SASE? To
be perfectly candid, I enclose an SASE if I'm particularly
anxious about a proposal or manuscript, knowing full well
that it's probably not necessary, but I'm not willing to risk
losing a job just because of the omission. Of course, if you
have included items with your query letter or manuscript
that you want returned, such as photographs, then it is necessary to include an SASE for their return. It is helpful to
attach a yellow "Post-It Note"™ to the envelope indicating
that it is to be used for the return of the photos and not the
entire package.

According to conventional wisdom, after six to eight weeks without a reply from the editor to whom you have sent a query letter or unsolicited manuscript, you should inquire about it. Again, I believe this is unwise advice. Follow-ups aren't worth the effort. You can be sure an editor will get back to you if he or she is interested in your work, but most query letters and manuscripts don't arouse interest and they simply hit the trash basket and aren't thought of again. Or, your query or manuscript could be stuck in a pile with other submissions and still be under consideration. I've learned that it doesn't help to make a follow-up call or send a letter to learn what has happened to a query letter or manuscript; you will hear from editors who are interested in your work. On the other hand, a manuscript that was written on assignment should certainly bring a response in the form of a check for payment. If you don't hear from an editor after fulfilling a contract, wait until the 15th of the following month, then write a note, indicate you have not been paid, and ask for prompt payment. Many businesses pay the past month's invoices during the first few days of the following month, and it's wise to grant this grace period before writing. It's easier to call, but smarter to create a paper trail by writing in the event that you need evidence of the communication.

PART III

GETTING BOOKS
PUBLISHED

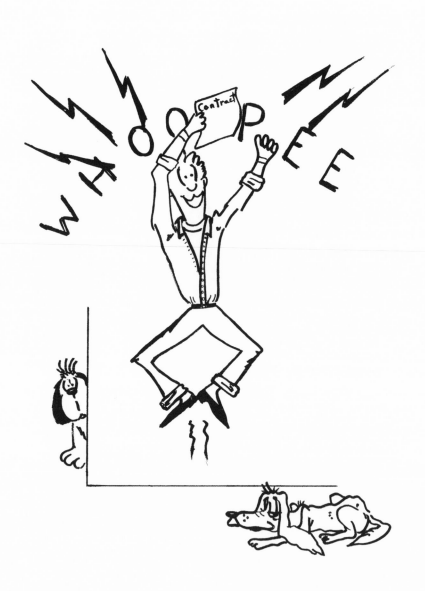

Chapter 9

LOCATING A
BOOK PUBLISHER

Do You Need An Agent?

Among the first issues to consider as you prepare to
find a publisher for a book manuscript is whether your
interests are best served by soliciting a publisher yourself
or by acquiring an agent to oversee the marketing
process. For reasons that will become abundantly clear,
most of you who are reading this book should go directly
to publishers with your manuscripts and not look for
agents to handle your work. Or, you can first *try* to find
an agent, and if that fails, then solicit a publisher on your
own.

This is how the solicitation system works for book manuscripts. Large publishers won't consider *fiction* submitted by authors; it MUST come to them through agents, while small to medium publishing houses regularly read unagented fiction. Most publishers, both large and small, consider *nonfiction* submitted by authors, but because agents have contacts at the large houses, their submissions are received more enthusiastically, and they are able to negotiate better contracts than authors can manage.

Around 75 percent of the books presented to publishers are submitted by agents, and nearly 90 percent of commercially successful books are handled by agents. They represent most celebrity authors and blockbuster books. You probably think, "Yes, that's for me," but if you aren't a celebrity, and if you are hoping to sell your first book, you probably won't have a blockbuster. Few agents will be knocking at your door.

Agents have a vested interest in representing only clients whose manuscripts have the potential to become books that will be big sellers because they receive a percent of the royalties their clients earn. Even though agents receive around 15 percent of the author's royalties for their services, an author can usually earn more by using an agent since the agent can attract better publishers and negotiate better contracts. In fact, many publishers have two printed contracts—one is used when negotiating with an author, and the other, with better terms, is used when negotiating with an agent.

Publishing houses that rely on agented manuscripts aren't interested in mid-list books (those that sell fewer than 20,000 copies); they want books that have the sales potential to amass large profits. This means agents aren't interested in handling the work of most fledgling writers. As you can see, you are caught in a "Catch 22" dilemma— it's difficult to get an agent unless you are a celebrity or until you have had a successful book published, and you have trouble attracting a large publisher without an agent. But all is not lost. With the big houses ignoring mid-list books as they search for commercial successes, an increasing number of small and medium size publishers are looking for solid, mid-list books, and your chance of getting into print through these publishers is greatly increased.

Locating a Book Publisher on Your Own

There are two obvious places to look for book publishers. One is among books already in print, whether these books are in your personal book collection, in public libraries, lining the shelves of bookstores, or listed in the reference book titled *Books In Print,* which is available in most libraries. By examining these books you will get a feel for the types of books various publishers produce. Make a list of the publishers that seem right for your material.

The other place to look for possible publishers is in marketing directories. The most widely used directories used to locate book publishers are *Writer's Market, Literary Market Place, Novel and Short Story Market,* and *International Directory Of Little Magazines and Small Presses.* These and other directories are listed on pages 258-260, along with descriptions of the books, their publishers, and addresses.

In Part II it was explained how to use directories to locate publishers of articles and short fiction. While some of the same marketing directories are used, the process of locating a book publisher is quite different. Some of the instructions that follow might seem redundant, but the procedure for locating a book publisher is explained in detail because important differences need to be pointed out.

Most marketing directories are large books listing thousands of publishers. The first place to turn as you begin your search is the "Book Publishers Subject Index." This index can facilitate identifying those publishers that print the type of manuscripts you write. The Subject Index lists the publishers of fiction and nonfiction separately. Nonfiction categories range from Agriculture to World Affairs, while fiction includes categories from Adventure to Westerns. Publishers may print books in a wide range of categories, and they are listed under each subject of their interest. Look up and study the complete listing for each publisher included in the category in which your manuscript might fit. These listings will provide valuable information about various publishers' interests and contractual arrangements. Compile a list of thirty to fifty publishers (that's right—thirty to fifty!) that seem appropriate for your work, and include any pertinent information that may affect your evaluation of a publisher. Rate each publisher as your search progresses, with the most desirable receiving a "10" and the least desirable receiving a "1."

Listings of publishing houses in marketing references will include the following information:

(1) The name and address of the publisher and editors.
Many editors may be listed for a given publisher. Sometimes the listing indicates the specialties of the editors, and of course, you should submit your work to the appropriate one. When many editors are listed, it can be helpful to phone the publishing house and ask a secretary to recommend an editor based on the subject of your manuscript. They are sometimes very helpful in this regard.

(2) Average number of titles printed each year and the number of submissions received.
This information indicates the amount of competition your manuscript will encounter. Study the submission/publication ratio and think about how your work might compete. These ratios range from fearsomely high to encouragingly low. While the numbers can be sobering, the odds aren't nearly as bad as those encountered at some periodicals where less than one article in 1500 submissions are printed. As you probably suspect, those with the most com-

petition are usually the larger and preferred publishers, while smaller publishers and those that concentrate on limited or specialty subjects receive fewer submissions.

The following brief list shows the range in the number of manuscripts several publishers receive each year and the percent of submissions that are published. It also shows the percent of manuscripts represented by agents compared to those that are not.

Publisher	Books Printed/ Submissions Ratio	Percent Published	Manuscript Source
William Morrow	250/10,000	2.5	95% Agented
			5% Unagented
HarperRow	150/10,000	1.5	50% Agented
			50% Unagented
Betterway	40/1200	3.3	10% Agented
			90% Unagented
Knowledge Book	5/75	6.6	100% Agented
Golden West Books	4/50	8.0	100% Unagented

The number of titles printed each year by the various publishing houses may range from hundreds to a mere three or four. Don't overlook the small presses, regional presses, or university presses, even though they may not put out an impressive number of titles. Many of these small operations are more adventurous and willing to take a risk on unpublished talent. Of course, the smaller presses don't have big budgets and can't spend much promoting their books, while the larger presses can spend a small fortune promoting some of their new publications (they usually reserve the big bucks for known names, and in a sense, they create best sellers through huge promotional campaigns). On the other hand, small to medium-size presses are inclined to keep books in print for many years, while some of the larger presses tend to drop those that fail to attract buyers quickly. It's a matter of weighing the advantages and disadvantages of the different publishers when deciding which to pursue, and then sometimes it's a matter of accepting the advances of the publisher that shows an interest in your manuscript. This is not a business for a prima donna waiting to be pursued.

(3) Kinds of material printed: fiction, nonfiction, texts, subjects of special interest, genre.
Solicit only those publishers that print the kind of manuscripts you produce. Read the listings very closely. While it may indicate, for example, that a publisher prints books about music, you need to determine what aspect of music is covered—history, performance, education, or some other niche in the music world. *Closely matching the subject of your manuscript with subjects that interest a publisher is perhaps the most important element in attracting a publisher.*

4) Kinds of books published: hardcover, trade paper-back, reprints, mass-market paperbacks.

You probably have an idea of how you want your work to appear in print. While you may not get what you want, first try to interest those publishers that produce the kinds of books you prefer. See a discussion of this subject on pages 19-21.

(5) Percent of submissions from agents and authors.

The percent of agented and unagented manuscripts printed varies among publishers, and you should consider this ratio when evaluating possible outlets for your work. Don't send your manuscript to publishers who only accept submissions from agents or to those who print a very low percentage of unagented work because it will be received with little excitement. Instead, concentrate on the mostly small to medium-sized publishers who prefer to work with unagented writers.

(6) Percent of books published by first-time authors.

Some publishers encourage and print new and unpub-lished writers while others aren't interested in taking the risk of publishing new talent. Don't bother soliciting the faint-hearted publisher.

(7) Payment.

The majority of book publishers offer a royalty on books sold, but some publishers pay higher royalties (a larger percentage of the sale price) than others.

A low percentage of publishers purchase manuscripts outright, and the author is paid a single lump sum regardless of whether the book becomes a best seller or only a few copies are sold. Writers usually prefer to take their chances and opt for royalty payments rather than selling their manuscripts and losing all control over them. If this is your feeling, avoid publishers who only print the manuscripts they purchase.

(8) Time between acceptance (contract) and publication.
Publishers usually print books and have them reach the market twice each year, in spring and fall. Generally, if an advance has been offered, a publisher will try to get the book to market quickly in order to recover some of the money invested in the project. Most books are in print within twelve to eighteen months after a contract is signed, although some publishers can get a book out within six to eight months. Others, especially small to medium presses, may take up to two years for publication.

In some cases, a contract is signed for a book that has yet to be written. The contract is offered on the basis of an outline and a few sample chapters. This rarely happens with fiction but is rather common with nonfiction subjects. Of course, most publishers are reluctant to enter into a contract with an unpublished writer based on an outline and a couple of chapters, but this is a routine and the preferred practice with established writers. The advantage of this arrangement is it allows the publisher more input into the direction, length, and design of the book. Obviously, it will take longer to get into print if the manuscript needs to be written after the contract is signed.

(9) Types of acceptable submissions.

Each listing will indicate if the editor or publisher wants to see a query letter, proposal, or a segment of the manuscript. Prepare your mailings accordingly. Query letters and proposals should be printed in the traditional manner, but with the availability of various electronic communication systems, manuscripts can be submitted in several ways. The majority of editors still prefer to receive manuscripts in hard copy (printed on paper, following their specified format). When using computer print-outs, be sure to tear off the perforated strip along each edge of the paper and separate the pages.

Some editors will accept, others prefer, electronic submissions, but before submitting material electronically, phone or write the publishing house to check for compatibility of equipment.

Listings also indicate if simultaneous submissions are acceptable. In the recent past, publishers adamantly refused to read simultaneous submissions, but now the practice has become more acceptable—even expected.

(10) Special instructions.

Some editors balk at reading dot matrix print-outs and indicate this in their listing. Others mention they don't want manuscripts printed with a justified right margin because they are more difficult to read. You may not understand why editors specify certain procedures, but follow their instructions precisely.

Writing a Query Letter or Proposal that Attracts Interest

Whether you are trying to sell your manuscript directly to a publisher or seeking an agent to represent you and your manuscript, your presentation will be essentially the same.

The terms "query" and "proposal" are sometimes used interchangeably but they are not the same. A "query" is a one-page letter that briefly explains the project and inquires if you might send a proposal. The one-page query letter should so stimulate an editor or agent that they will ask you to send a proposal. The letter should include:

(1) A paragraph or two about the subject of the book and why it should be published.

(2) A market analysis explaining how the book you propose will differ from those already on the market.

(3) A brief description of your background and why you are qualified to write the book.

(4) The length of the proposed manuscript. Some publishers are willing to publish voluminous tomes, but most are interested in medium-length books of 80,000 to 120,000

words. It's practically impossible for an unpublished writer to find a publisher for a very long book because they are more expensive to produce, and publishers are unwilling to invest too much in an unknown writer.

(5) Indicate the number of photos and illustrations you plan to include. Line drawings and black and white photos are not too expensive to reproduce but the printing of high quality color photos dramatically increases the cost of production and will surely influence the decision on whether or not to consider the manuscript for publication. Of course, some publishers concentrate on visual books while others favor books with few or no pictures.

(6) Be sure to mention when you can complete the manuscript and that you are willing to consider the editor's suggestions so as to produce a useful and marketable book. Editors are impressed with such a statement because it suggests you are aware of their needs and goals and will be easy to work with.

Polish your query letter as if it is the most important thing you've ever written. It may be. Without a powerful query letter, your manuscript won't get into print; your career rests on being able to write a compelling and persuasive letter. Be sure to include an SASE with each book query letter you send. According to a survey conducted by *Writers Digest,* 35 percent of the responding editors said they discard book queries that do not include SASEs. See the sample book query letter below. Query letters must be no longer than a single page. This letter, while it appears lengthy, can be printed on a single sheet of 8 1/2 x 11 inch paper.

                    Use printed letterhead

Date

Alan Turner, Editor
CHILTON PUBLISHING COMPANY
Radnor, Pennsylvania 19089

Dear Mr. Turner:

             WORKING AT HOME MAKES
               DOLLARS AND SENSE

    I have begun to write a manuscript for
a book about how to start and sustain a
home business and how a home business
affects a household. I am looking for a
publisher before the organization of the
manuscript is finalized. With statistics
showing a growing number of women (and
men) becoming dissatisfied with leaving
their children to be raised in childcare
centers while they pursue careers, and a

resurgence in the growth of home businesses, the time is ripe to publish a
new book that explains how one goes
about setting up shop at home. The manuscript I am writing explores the potential for home businesses based on traditional jobs, as well as those that have
been created as a result of the development of computers and sophisticated communications equipment.

The book I propose will be different
from those currently on the market. It
will explore not only how to operate a
business, but also how to mesh family,
home, and business to yield a satisfying
lifestyle.

I am qualified to write the proposed
book. My daughter, husband, and I operate a cottage industry, Printed Tree,
Inc. We manufacture giftware, with labor
provided by others in their homes, and
we sell our products through sales reps
throughout the United States. I am a
small business consultant, conduct seminars, and have given many lectures on
the subject of home businesses and working from home. Also, I write regularly

and have had several articles on this subject published in national periodicals.

I visualize a book of approximately 100,000 words, illustrated with both b/w photographs and line drawings. I do my own artwork and photography. I am flexible on the content and format of the book, willing to act upon my editor's suggestions and to include or exclude subjects in order to produce a useful and marketable book.

If you would like to see a complete proposal with an outline and sample chapters, I will be happy to forward it to you.

I look forward to hearing from you.

Sincerely,

Jo Frohbieter-Mueller

A *proposal* includes (1) a letter, (2) an outline or table of contents, (3) a chapter or two of written text, (4) a more thorough market analysis, (5) samples of illustrations and photos you plan to use, (6) your résumé, and (7) an SASE. Let's take a closer look at each of these components.

(1) The letter you send with a proposal is similar to the query letter you sent earlier, but it can be longer than a single page. It should include a brief synopsis of the proposed book, indicate the target market, the length and when the manuscript can be completed, explain why you are qualified to write the manuscript, and any other information that is pertinent to the project.

(2) The outline or table of contents should contain enough details for the editor to understand what you plan to cover. As you probably know, a detailed and well-organized outline is the backbone of anything you write, and it's well worth spending considerable time refining it. An editor can tell if you have a good grasp of a subject by the outline you produce.

(3) When considering a proposal, an editor needs to know how you handle data and your writing style. Select a segment of text that flows like sand, one in which you have incorporated an intriguing piece of information, or maybe used a perfect quote that succinctly makes a point. Make sure the segment captures the essence of the larger project, whether it's a deftly crafted vignette or an explanation of a complicated concept.

(4) A thorough market analysis. This should include a brief description of competing books, indicating when and by whom they were published. This information is available in the reference, *Books In Print.*

(5) Samples of illustrations and photos. Send copies of a few of the illustrations and photos that will be included in the book; never send the originals.

(6) A résumé. Include a résumé containing only pertinent information. Nobody cares where you went to school or the various and sundry jobs you have had unless this information is relevant to the manuscript you are trying to sell.

With the query letter and proposal prepared, it's time to use the list of possible publishers you compiled as you studied your writer's marketing directories. Remember, send only the type of material asked for in the listing— either a query letter or a complete proposal.

Finding a publisher is chancy and unpredictable. You might find one with your first mailing, but more than likely, you'll need to contact several or many publishers before locating one who wants to print your manuscript. It could take a long time to find a publisher if you submit a query or proposal to one or two publishers at a time because some don't reply for months. For this reason, *you should send a query letter and/or a proposal to at least six publishers simultaneously.* If for one reason or another you think your manuscript will be difficult to sell, send twenty or more queries out simultaneously. Keep sending out query letters and proposals, replacing each rejection you get with a new submission. Work down the list of possible publishers that you have prepared, sending first to those you rated "10," and continuing through the list until you get a bite.

What Happens at the Publishing House?

Understanding how a submission is handled can help you prepare one that will be well-received. The first mailing, either a single page query letter or a letter with supporting materials, will land on the desk of the editor to whom it is addressed. This editor will read the submission, and if interested, ask you to send more material.

When an editor expresses interest in seeing more material, follow instructions precisely. Some may want to see a few chapters; others may want the complete manuscript or as much as you have prepared. If you feel more information is needed to explain the project, include it in the accompanying cover letter.

The editor who receives your material will review it and make a judgment about its value to the publishing house. Editors at small publishing firms sometimes have the authority to offer a contract on the basis of their analysis, but most editors at medium to large publishing houses lack this authority. Instead, the editor who has been favorably impressed with your submission will present it to an editorial board. Depending on the publishing house, editorial board meetings are held every week, month, or quarter, with the editorial and marketing staffs present. It is here that the fate of your proposal is decided. Prior to the meeting, the sponsoring editor might solicit the support of another editor if he or she is especially excited about the project, and these editors will function as your advocate before the editorial board. Many questions will be asked about the proposed book in an effort to determine whether or not the publishing house can make an adequate profit on the proposed title. Factors that must be considered are, (1) Who will buy the book, (2) The size of the potential audience, (3) Books on the same subject already in print and how the proposed book differs from them. You will certainly want to provide this information. Other factors that will be discussed at the editorial meeting are your qualifications for writing the book, your ability as a writer, the cost of producing the book, the price that can be charged for it, and the size of the first run. If it is concluded that the proposal can yield a profitable book, the sponsoring editor will notify you, and you will be offered a contract.

Negotiating a Contract

Beginning writers tend to think a contract is to be signed and returned, no questions asked, but many items in a contract are negotiable. Publishers expect changes to be made, and now is the time to sharpen your negotiating skills. There are several issues to consider.

Should You Seek an Advance?

Many publishers offer an advance against anticipated earnings. An advance is money paid to an author after a contract is signed but before the book is published. The amount of the advance will be deducted from royalties earned by the author. If book sales fail to cover the amount of the advance, the author does not need to reimburse the publisher for the loss.

Some publishers offer many thousands of dollars as an advance while others offer nothing. The size of an advance offered by the larger publishers is approximately the amount the publisher expects the author to earn in royalties from the first printing or during the first year after publication. This amount is determined by multiplying the number of books by the price of the book and the royalty rate. If 10,000 books are printed, each selling for $10, with a royalty of 5 percent, then the advance would be $5000 (10,000 X $10 = $100,000 X 5% = $5000). Medium-sized publishers don't follow this formula; they set their own rate based on individual cases. An advance of $500 to $2000 is what you might expect, while very small publishers rarely offer anything.

Advances are paid in several ways. If the book is completed, the advance might be paid in full at the time the contract is signed, or half of the amount might be paid at that time and the remaining half paid on publication. If the book has not been completed, half of the advance could be given at the time the contract is signed and the other half when the completed manuscript is delivered. Or, one third might be given at the time the contract is signed, another third when the manuscript is delivered, and the final third is paid on publication. It may not seem like an advance if it is paid on publication, but remember, it will take another six to nine months after publication before the author receives any royalties from sales.

The purpose of an advance is twofold. The most obvious purpose is it provides income while the author is writing the manuscript, but there is an equally important reason for seeking an advance. An advance is an investment made by the publisher in the book under contract, and in order to recover their investment, the publisher must get the book on the market where it can generate sales. You might think of an advance as earnest money—an expression by the publisher that your work will be published. Without an advance, the publisher has no binding commitment to get a manuscript into print; should a better manuscript come along, the contract and the promise of getting published could be pushed aside. So try to get an advance.

What Kind of Royalties Can You Expect?

Royalties for standard mass paperbacks range from 4 to 8 percent of the net price. Royalties for standard hardcover books are usually around 10 percent of the net price on the first 5,000 copies sold, and increase to 12 1/2 percent for the next 5,000 and 15 percent thereafter. Royalties for trade paperback books are no less than 6 percent of the retail (list) price on the first 20,000 copies with an increase to 7 1/2 percent thereafter. However, these are flexible and negotiable. For instance, if a book contains a lot of photos, it will be very expensive to produce, and the publisher may offer a lower royalty.

How Many Books are Planned for the First Printing?

The size of the first printing suggests how the publisher views the prospects for your book. A publisher who plans a small first printing, say 500 copies, surely has reservations about the book's market potential. Many publishers only print 3,000 to 5,000 copies of an author's first book but print more if the book sells well. If possible, avoid publishers who plan a very small first printing.

Costs to Author

There can be hidden or unexpected costs as a publisher converts a manuscript into a printed book. Publishers cover most of these costs. A contract should clearly spell out any costs to be borne by the author. You may need to pay for permission to use something that has appeared in print, and sometimes the author must pay for photographic work. You shouldn't pay for illustrations produced by the publisher's staff, but you will be expected to pay for costs that result from changes you make in the text after it has been set in type, if those costs are excessive. Prior to setting type, you will have the opportunity to make any changes you deem necessary. When the manuscript is typeset, you will be provided galley sheets and will be expected to study them carefully for errors. Typesetting errors and formatting errors will incur costs that are borne by the publisher. However, if you make extensive changes in the text, the cost may be passed on to you.

Author/Publisher Contract

The following contract includes the main points generally addressed in author/publisher contracts, but changes can be made to accommodate specific projects.

An agreement dated (date), between (Name of publisher) hereafter referred to as the Publisher and (Name of Author(s) of (Address of Author(s), hereafter referred to as the Author(s), for rights to publish, and to license subsequent publications or other utilization by third parties, of a written manuscript tentatively entitled (Name of Book), hereafter referred to as the Work.

1. The Author hereby grants to the publisher exclusive rights to publish and sell said Work in book form, in the English language, in the United States of America (and elsewhere in the world where publishing rights may be granted by the Publisher). [The statement in parenthesis may be added if agreed to by both parties.]

2. The Author additionally grants to the Publisher the right to license third parties to publish and/or sell distinct editions of said work in book form, newspaper or magazine serial forms, condensation, partial extract, in English or in translation into another language, in all areas of the world included in the previous paragraph, in return for which rights, the Publisher agrees to pay to the Author 50% of all royalties received by the Publisher from said third parties for such licensing.

3. The Author additionally grants to the publisher the exclusive right to license third parties to transfer all or

part of the Work to sound recording, film, videotape, electronic computing media, Braille, photographic prints, or dramatic adaptations, for which rights the Publisher agrees to pay the Author 80% of all royalties received by the Publisher from said third parties for said licensing.

4. This agreement shall be binding on both Author and Publisher for as long as a registered copyright to said work remains in force, and upon their respective heirs, administrators, successors and assigns, unless terminated by written agreement of all parties, or as specifically provided for elsewhere in this agreement or in the U.S. Copyright Act of 1976.

5. The Author agrees to provide a completed manuscript of said work, conforming in all essential respects to the concept of the work represented to the Publisher on the date of this agreement, no later than (date). The Author further agrees to provide such illustrative and other supplemental material as shall have been included in that prior concept

of the work, and permission for any inclusion of material copyrighted by others, at the Author's expense, no later than (<u>date</u>), except for the following material and permissions which are to be obtained by the Publisher, at the Publisher's expense:

_____

_____

6. The Publisher agrees to pay to the Author, as an advance guarantee, to be deducted from subsequently-earned royalties, the sum of $_____, one-third of which will be paid on signing of this agreement, one-third of which will be paid on delivery to the publisher of the completed manuscript, and one-third of which will be paid on completion of such suggested prepublication manuscript revisions as are acceptable to both Author and Publisher.

7. Prior to publication of said work, the Publisher shall provide to the Author one set of proofs of the typographical composition of the work, and shall agree to correct any discrepancies between said proof and the edited manu-

script at no cost to the Author. Additional changes in the proof will be made only if acceptable to both Author and Publisher, with the cost of such changes as are proposed by the Author to be deducted from subsequent royalties due the Author. [Or, the Author might be charged for changes that cost, for instance, more than 5% to 10% of the typesetting cost.] Upon publication of each distinct edition of the work, the Publisher shall provide to the Author, without cost, ten finished copies of the work, and shall agree to sell to the Author additional copies at a price equaling 60% of the announced list price of the edition involved, as long as that edition remains in stock.

8. A clear accounting of all money received by the Publisher from sales of this work in book form, or from licensing of rights for utilization of the work by others, shall be provided by the Publisher to the Author within six months after the first receipt of any such income, and at intervals of not more than six months thereafter, with the condition that such accountings

shall cover a period ending no more than
30 days before the date of each accounting. Payment of all royalties due the
Author, after subtraction of previously-
paid advances or typographical alter-
ation costs for which the Author is
liable, shall be made in full at time of
each such accounting unless other terms
of payment have been accepted prior to
said accounting by both Author and Publisher, except that the publisher may
withhold up to 7% of royalties due as a
margin to cover possible merchandise
returns, if the publisher deems such
withholding advisable.

9. Complete responsibility for any
infringement by plagiarism, libel, slander, or other means, of the rights of
others by material included in the original manuscript shall be borne by the
Author. Responsibility for such infringe-
ments by supplementary material provided
by the Publisher shall be borne by the
Publisher.

10. In the event of discontinuation of
publishing operations by the Publisher,
all rights transferred to the Publisher

by this agreement shall revert to the
Author.

11. Any dispute between the parties to
this agreement which involves interpretation of the terms of the agreement
shall be submitted to arbitration under
the rules of the American Arbitration
Association, and the findings of the
Arbitrator shall be binding on all parties. Any other dispute concerning fulfillment of this agreement shall be litigated in a court of competent
jurisdiction. Legal interpretation of
this agreement shall be governed by the
laws of the state in which the Publisher
is domiciled.

12. Other provisions agreed to by all
parties are:

[These are typed in, rather than a
part of the printed document, and might
include something like the following:]

Publisher agrees to pay Author royalties on all monies actually received
from sales of Work, as follows:

```
1 - 9999 copies              10%
10,000 - 19,999 copies       12%
20,000 - 29,999 copies       14%
30,000 copies and more       16%
```

Royalty payments described in paragraph 2 shall be made on all subsidiary rights sales including, but not limited to, abridgements, excerpts, and book clubs.

13. This contract is the only and entire agreement between above-named Publisher and Author(s) concerning the Work identified herein.

14. This contract will be considered valid only if signed and returned no later than (<u>date</u>).

Signed:

Publisher,date: _____

Author,date: _____

(Two copies are signed; one is returned to the publisher, the other retained by the author.)

Chapter 10

USING A LITERARY AGENT TO SELL YOUR MANUSCRIPT

Functions of an Agent

Literary agents have become important liaisons between authors and publishers. They are of value to authors because they find publishers for their work. Agents oversee contract negotiations and collect and forward royalties to their clients. With increasing opportunities in television, films, and foreign publications, an agent's expertise is needed to reserve rights for future sales in these media, and they solicit these subsidiary sales for their clients. Some agents offer editorial and critiquing services, and they work with editors as their clients' books are being produced, serving as a buffer between the author and the editor.

Literary agents are of value to publishers because they screen manuscripts and direct them to the publishers most appropriate for the work. They function as first readers, thus reducing the cost of hiring readers at the publishing houses. An agent gains the confidence and respect of editors by carefully screening manuscripts and matching them with the right publishers. To be effective, an agent must be able to evaluate a manuscript, know the market and the type of material the major publishers handle, and have contacts and working relations with editors within the major publishing houses. Agents who become known as poor judges of manuscripts quickly lose access to the editors and are of no value to their clients.

The following statistics, compiled from questionnaires completed by members of Literary Agents of North America and gleaned from a variety of marketing directories, can help you understand a little about how agents work.

- 88% of agents have less than 100 clients.

- 89% read unsolicited queries and proposals from unpublished writers.

- 78% won't read unsolicited manuscripts.

- 68% do no editorial work but refer writers to outside editors (for this, the agent may receive a commission).

- 95% of the agents who provide editorial services charge fees.

- 61% provide ghostwriters or collaborators.

- 45% read novelettes and short story collections.

- 93% will not handle articles or fiction for magazines, although agents occasionally represent magazine articles or fiction for clients whose books they represent.

- Just a few agents handle collections of poetry, 37% handle juvenile literature, 26% work with professional books, and less than 10% represent textbooks.

- There is a large turnover in the agency business, with over one-fourth of those listed in marketing directories being listed for the first time.

Locating and Evaluating Agents

The procedure used to locate an agent to represent your work is similar to that used to locate a publisher to print it.

Agents are listed in several reference books including *Literary Market Place, Writer's Market Literary Agents,* and *Writer's Handbook*. The latter is published in England but includes U.S. agents as well. Other directories are listed on page 260. Depending on the reference used, literary agencies are listed in the directories in the following ways: alphabetical order, size index, geographical index, personnel index and, most importantly, subject index.

The subject index is divided into two sections, fiction and nonfiction. The fiction section lists agents according to the genre they represent. The nonfiction listing identifies the subjects and the kinds of books the agents represent— juvenile, texts, how-tos, and so forth. When trying to locate an agent, use the subject index first. This index will lead you to the agents who handle the kind of manuscripts you produce. Just as publishers have individual listings in marketing directories, so do literary agents. These listings provide valuable information and should be studied closely as you try to match your work with the appropriate agent.

The listings in *Writer's Market Literary Agents* include the following information:

(1) Name and address of the agent or agency.

(2) Number of clients represented.
Some years ago writers wanted large agencies in New York City representing them, but now many prefer small agencies located closer to home. Smaller agencies generally provide more guidance than those in New York, some

of which are not interested in taking on a writer whose writing income is less that $25,000 yearly. According to Michael Larson, in his book *Literary Agents: How to Get and Work with the Right One for You*, new and small agencies bring an enthusiasm and passion to projects and are often preferred to the more sophisticated New York agents who are looking for a quick sale and a fast buck. Don't pass up an agency just because it's a one person operation because sometimes these people succeed on the enthusiasm they bring to their work.

(3) The agent's policy on reading and reporting time.

Some agencies read all comers, while others read only manuscripts they have asked to see after having first seen a query letter and/or a proposal on the project. Always start your search by sending query letters or proposals rather than full manuscripts. Reporting time on query letters and proposals varies from a week to a month or two (occasionally an agent will respond within a few days), while reporting time for complete manuscripts runs anywhere from two weeks to rarely longer than three months.

(4) Kinds of material handled.

Look for a close match between your manuscript and an agent's interest. Earlier in this section, I mentioned that the most important factor in finding a publisher for your manuscript is in matching the subject and style of the manuscript with the appropriate publisher. The same principle holds true when soliciting an agent.

5) Terms.

The commission charged by agents runs from 10 to 20 percent of the royalties earned by the author for the manuscripts they place with publishers. The royalty payment is sent to the agent, and the commission is deducted before the remainder of the royalty is forwarded to the author. Agents usually get 20 percent for foreign sales and movie or television sales, but this may be split with another agent who has access to the foreign publishers or film editors and who may actually make the sale.

(6) Fees charged.

Most agencies read query letters and proposals at no charge, but some charge a fee to read a manuscript. Be aware of these fees before submitting a manuscript; they are noted in the listings. Some agencies earn a large portion of their income through reading and critiquing fees, and then, after having worked on a manuscript, they may not accept it for representation. You may want to avoid these agencies unless, of course, you need a critiquing service. Chances are, if you need this service, you aren't ready to get into print but need to hone your writing skills a while longer.

Some agencies charge fees for consultation, typing, handling, and editorial work. There are agents who subcontract work to free-lance editors who, for a hefty fee, overhaul manuscripts without the assurance that the agent will handle the work after it has been revised. Be wary of agents whose listings indicate they earn a large percent of their income through reading and editorial fees because some of them fill their pockets with an assortment of fees, but then limit their marketing efforts.

If a manuscript needs heavy editing, an agent may give the client the option of either paying for the editing or paying a larger percent of the royalties (up to 25 percent) for services rendered (which would include editing and selling the manuscript). An agent willing to accept a higher commission, rather than payment up front for editorial work, suggests the agent thinks the work will sell and the money will be recovered. Therefore, if you can afford it, you would be better off paying a single editorial fee and giving the agent a lower percentage of royalties you receive from sales.

After signing a contract with an agent, you can expect to pay a few fees before your work is distributed to potential publishers, especially if you are unpublished. Around 85 percent of the agencies ask for a little money to cover marketing expenses since they have out-of-pocket expenses just getting a manuscript prepared and sent to various publishing houses. Depending on the agency, the fee may cover postage, messenger service, long-distance phone calls, and photocopying. Never agree to pay an agent travel expenses or a retainer. The just-to-get-started fee usually runs between $50 and $100, and some agencies reimburse the writer for the fee when the manuscript is sold; others do not. Agencies usually forgo marketing fees for clients who have successful books in print.

(7) Recent sales.
Agents list their most important sales to demonstrate

how successful they have been because writers are looking for agents who can place books with big publishers or ones who have had previous successes. The "Recent Sales" section for many listings read, "No information given," or, "Confidential." This may mean that these agents haven't sold any books—or at least they haven't sold any they are willing to admit to having sold (maybe they represented books that were slow to sell after they were published). These may be new agents or agents who derive income primarily from reading and editorial fees—not from finding publishers for client's books. It's best to avoid listings that don't include names of recent sales.

It may surprise you to learn that agents can be included in marketing references without showing evidence of success. They can say they are in business and be listed; these people may have had no prior training, no contacts within the industry, no experience, and no successes. This leaves the writers who are looking for agents in a somewhat precarious position as they search the listings, and this is reason enough to read between the lines of these listings. It may also be reason enough to favor agents who belong to one of several agent organizations. Membership in these organizations suggests commitment, and most of these organizations have a code of ethics their members are expected to follow. These organizations include:

ILAA—Independent Literary Agents Association, Inc. Suite 1205, 432 Park Ave., S., New York, NY 10016. Send an SASE for a list of members and a copy of the organization's code of ethics. The membership consists of agents who have sold at least twelve titles in the last eighteen months and includes many small and relatively new agents.

SAR—Society of Author's Representatives, Inc. 10 S. Portland Ave., Brooklyn, NY 11217. This society is composed mainly of New York agents from larger and older firms. Send an SASE for a membership list and procedural brochure.

WGA—Writers Guild of America includes writers and agents. Members are required to sign an agreement concerning standards in business practices and the treatment of clients. For a list of members, send a money order for $1.25. If your address is east of the Mississippi write to WGA East, 555 W. 57th St., New York, NY 10019. Those living west of the Mississippi should write WGA West, 8955 Beverly Blvd., Los Angeles, CA 90048.

Of course, many agents don't belong to any organization and are just as effective as the organized agents at finding publishers for their clients. For this reason, it is particularly important to study the "Recent Sales" category as you evaluate the agent listings.

Soliciting an Agent

As mentioned earlier, it is sometimes as difficult for an unknown writer to obtain a literary agent as it is for an unknown writer to get a book published, but if you want your manuscript printed by a publisher who only considers agented work, then you must find an agent to represent you. Many agents are reluctant to take on newcomers because their manuscripts are usually difficult to place. This leaves the new writer scrambling for representation. Fortunately, there are agents who willingly look at all query letters they receive, knowing that there are many good writers waiting to be discovered. With patience and persistence you will uncover those who are ready and willing and develop a healthy partnership.

Follow the accepted procedure when soliciting an agent. First, send a query letter or a proposal to at least six agents *who represent the kind of material you write*. The listing of each agent will indicate the preferred submission. The query letter and proposal is essentially like the one you would send if you were soliciting a publisher (see page 149), except they should indicate you are seeking agent representation. If you are seeking representation for a non-fiction manuscript, the proposal should include a one-page letter, an outline, a chapter or two of text, and an SASE; a synopsis and at least three chapters of text should be sent if you are soliciting an agent to represent fiction. By the way, never hire a professional service to write a query letter because the agent will learn of this deception when you submit your manuscript. Always keep at least six query letters and/or proposals in the pipeline, replacing each rejection with another submission to a different agent.

When an agent expresses interest and asks to see your manuscript, follow instructions exactly. They usually want to see a neat, proofed copy with ample margins. And, by all means, get it into the mail quickly. While one agent is reading your manuscript, continue to send query letters and proposals to other agents, and forward a copy of your manuscript to each who expresses interest. You may eventually have copies of your manuscript in the hands of several agents.

Give each agent about two months to read the manuscript and reply. If you haven't heard from them within three months, write or phone to learn what is causing the delay. You probably won't want to sign with an agent who works so slowly, so unless there is a good reason for the delay, you might as well cross that agent off your list of potential agents and continue your search.

You will be rejected—you can count on that—and that is why you need to keep up the marketing process even though one or several agents are reading your manuscript.

Don't give up your search on the basis of a few rejections. Most agents represent fewer than a hundred clients, yet they receive thousands of queries, proposals, and unsolicited manuscripts each year, so it's not surprising that they turn down most manuscripts that cross their desks. Nonetheless, if your manuscript is well-written and on a subject that will interest publishers, with persistence and determination, you will find an agent to represent it.

As you solicit an agent, you can expect to exchange several letters and maybe call each other a couple of times before signing a contract. Read between the lines of each communication. Be alert for indications that the agent appreciates your manuscript and believes in your ability. *Avoid an agent who is willing to accept you as a client without having read your work.* You want an agent who represents excellent authors because only then will that agent have the respect of the editors at the publishing houses. That respect is needed to sell manuscripts. You'd like to know as much as possible about an agent before signing away control of your manuscript, but many are annoyed if you ask for a client list unless you can provide an impressive list of titles that you have had published. Consequently, you have no choice but to bite your tonque and base your judgment on the overall feel you get from your communications.

Signing an Agreement

This is a big step. You must make sure you are signing with an agent who is sensitive to the type of material you write and one who has shown, through previous sales, that he or she has the contacts needed to produce good contracts.

How can you know if an agent is right for you? After you have communicated with several agents in your search, you will start to get a feel for what it is you are seeking. There is a sort of chemistry that develops, and you'll know it when it happens. You will find you can talk with one agent but feel stressed or uneasy when talking with others. One may show genuine excitement when talking about your manuscript. You need that. You need to trust your agent, and only sign an agreement when you feel the agent has your best interest at heart. Of course, agents also have their own best interests at heart, but fortunately, the two go hand in hand. When your agent attracts a good publisher and a good contract, both you and the agent win.

You need a written contract that defines the agreement between you and your agent. A few agents still work with verbal agreements, but a printed contract is the best arrangement. It protects both you and the agent, and there is little room for misunderstandings or disagreements because terms and procedures are spelled out. Most agents have a standard printed contract they expect their clients to sign, but if something in the contract doesn't set well with you, it is probably negotiable and you should work with the agent to resolve your differences. Don't try to pick the contract to pieces. I recall a writer whom I had decided to accept as a client. At contract signing time, he challenged virtually every item on the contract and acted as though I was his adversary. Obviously, the man didn't trust me, and I told him to look elsewhere for representation. At the minimum, the contract should specify the agreed fees and terms and what rights are for sale. Among other items, it should define what happens if the work isn't sold within a specified period of time, or if the work is sold but the author fails to produce a completed manuscript. Study the sample contract at the end of this chapter.

After signing an agreement with an agent, do what you can to help the agent solicit a publisher. You might provide a second copy of the manuscript because they quickly become shopworn, and a fresh copy is needed when approaching a new publisher. Agents frequently make several or many submissions simultaneously in order to speed up the sale of a manuscript, and anything you can provide the agent that will ease the task of multiple submissions will be appreciated.

After signing with an agent, *you must not do any marketing on your own*; all marketing will be handled by your agent. Yes, in a sense you lose control of the destiny of your manuscript, and, for this reason, you must have faith in your agent. Get busy with other projects and try not to think about the work being done on your behalf because it may take several months, or more, to make a sale. You will be better off if you have other things occupying your mind.

Sometimes an agent accepts a client and seems to be excited about the project, but nothing happens. The author may become concerned that nothing is being done with the manuscript. That's a legitimate concern. While the author has a lot to lose if a manuscript isn't sold, the agent has little at risk. Seek a progress report. Where has your manuscript been sent, and what kinds of responses is the agent getting? After learning of the marketing effort, you may decide the agent isn't doing the job, and when the contract permits, you may wish to end the relationship and seek other representation. On the other hand, the agent could be working very hard on your behalf, but to no avail. Remember, you are just one of many clients, and you will get better service if you are patient and pleasant rather than rude and demanding when talking or writing to your agent. If your agent is actively pursuing a publisher, you should probably "hang in there" and not threaten to "jump ship." If you decide you *must* change agents, it's important to learn which publishers have seen the manuscript, so your new agent can analyze the marketing background and not solicit the same publishers.

When a possible publisher is located, the publisher and your agent will haggle over a contract. The agent will go after the best terms, biggest advance, largest first printing possible, while still saving some of the rights for future sales. After coming to terms with a publisher, your agent will contact you to learn if the arrangement is acceptable. Unless you have serious reservations, take the advice of your agent and accept the contract.

```
        Sample Author/Agent Contract


    An agreement dated  _____
between [name of agent or agency, name of
officer of agency, address of agency],
hereafter referred to as the Agent, and
```

[name of author], hereafter referred to as Author. This agreement gives the Agent the right to solicit on behalf of the Author, a publisher for a manuscript, tentatively titled, [insert name of manuscript], hereafter referred to as the Work.

1. The Author hereby grants to the Agent exclusive rights to sell said Work to a publisher, but the Author has the right to refuse to accept a publisher he/she deems inadequate or inappropriate for the Work.

2. The Author agrees to pay the Agent 15% of all monies actually received from the publisher for sales of said Work, plus expenses incurred in locating and completing the contract between Publisher and Agent. The Author will deposit $50 with the Agent to cover solicitation costs (postage, telephone calls, and copying fees). Whether the book is, or is not sold, any money left over from the deposit will be refunded to the Author. An accounting of these expenditures will be provided to the Author.

3. The Author additionally grants to the Agent the right to work with a publisher in seeking other parties to publish and/or sell distinct editions of said Work in book form, newspaper or magazine serial form, condensation, partial extract, in English or in translation into another language, in all

areas of the world, for which the Agent will receive 15% of the monies actually received from publisher for the sales of the Work.

4. The Author additionally grants to the Agent the exclusive right to license third parties to transfer all or part of the Work to sound recordings, film, videotape, electronic computing media, Braille, photographic prints, or dramatic adaptations, for which the Agent will receive 15% of the monies actually received from the publisher for the sales of the Work.

5. If the Work has not been sold within one year of the signing of this contract, the contract can be canceled by either party by mailing a certified or registered letter to that effect. After the manuscript has been sold to a publisher, this agreement shall be binding on both Author and Agent for as long as a registered copyright to said Work remains in force, and upon their respective heirs, administrators, successors and assigns, unless terminated by written agreement of all parties, or as specifically provided for elsewhere in this agreement or in the U.S. Copyright Act of 1976.

6. The Author agrees to provide a completed manuscript within the time limit agreed upon between Publisher, Agent and

Author. In the event said manuscript is not provided to the Publisher via the Agent by said date, the Author shall refund within 30 days any monies paid by the Publisher as an advance against royalties, including the 15% retained by the Agent. However, the Publisher has the option to extend the manuscript completion date, whereupon the advance can be retained by the Author.

7. A clear accounting of all monies received by the Publisher, and submitted to the Agent, from the sales of this work shall be provided to the Author within one month after receipt. Payment of all royalties due the Author, after subtraction of 15% Agent's fee, shall be paid in full at the time of each accounting.

8. Complete responsibility for any infringement, by plagiarism, libel, slander, or other means, of the rights of others by material included in the manuscript shall be borne by the Author.

9. Any dispute between the parties to this agreement, which involves interpretation of the terms of the agreement, shall be submitted to arbitration under the rules of the American Arbitration Association, and the findings of the Arbitrator shall be binding on all parties. Any other dispute

concerning fulfillment of this agreement shall be litigated in a court of competent jurisdiction. Legal interpretation of this agreement shall be governed by the laws of the state in which the Agent or Author is domiciled.

10. This contract is the only and entire agreement between the named Author and Agent concerning the Work identified herein, as of the contract date above.

Signed

_____

(Agent)   (Date)

_____

(Author)   (Date)

_____

(Address of Author)

Chapter 11

OTHER WAYS TO
GET INTO PRINT

Many writers are unable to interest either a publisher or an agent in their manuscripts, so they turn to other methods to get into print. The following options are for writers who are willing to financially support the publication of their work, or for those who have received a grant or some other form of financial backing to get their manuscript printed. This sometimes occurs when the subject matter is of interest to a defined group, such as the history of a church or a small community. In these cases, the publication is usually subsidized by the organization and distributed to its members. For a variety of reasons, the following methods of publication need to be approached with caution and with an awareness of the advantages and disadvantages inherent in each of them.

189

Self-Publishing is an Option

Desktop publishing has made self-publishing a national pastime. Desktop publishing means using a personal computer, in combination with text, graphics, and page layout programs to produce publication-quality documents. Rather than making the rounds of publishers and agents, some writers are cranking out their manuscripts on home computers, using layout features from desktop publishing programs such as Pagemaker, Ventura, or Quark. The term "desktop publishing" is misleading because multiple copies of documents do not come pouring out of the printer. Instead, these programs produce printer-ready copy. To produce a book, the sheets are printed and bound. Others pursue the self-publishing route by having their manuscripts typeset by commercial printers, after which the pages are printed and bound. This is much more expensive than desktop publishing. While some of the books produced by these methods look "homemade," others are "slicker" and better produced, but they rarely have the finished quality of books produced by regular publishing houses because they lack the attention of experienced editors and layout artists.

Still, there are times when self-publishing is the best way to get into print. This is true if a manuscript is of interest to a limited number of people. For instance, a family history or some personal poems you want to share with family and friends would not be suitable material for regular publishers, but you might be willing to pay for the printing and binding of such a book.

Sometimes a writer can actually earn a profit through self-publishing, but this usually happens only when a network or outlet for book sales already exists. An acquaintance of mine, Brad Chaffin, suffered from multiple sclerosis. This man (who has now succumbed to the disease) possessed remarkable skill, will, and goodwill. Among his other accomplishments is the book *Creative Living with MS*. Brad had neither the considerable time nor energy needed to find a publisher, so he self-published his book. He found a printer, did his own layout, and got his ideas into print. A professional could have produced a better book by closer editing and by selecting more appropriate fonts and format, but Brad knew he had a market for his book and was willing to take the risk of self-publishing. Brad was active in the National Multiple Sclerosis Society and was acquainted with many people suffering from MS. As a result of his work with the Society, he had access to their mailing list and advertised his book through the Society's newsletter. This was a natural marketing vehicle, and Brad made a modest profit from his efforts. But more importantly, he was able to share some valuable tips with other MS sufferers about how to get more out of life.

Another case illustrates the wisdom of self-publishing. A professor of theatre wanted his book printed by a commercial publisher, but when he failed to attract one, he self-published and now uses the book in his classroom. With each student buying a copy, he is gradually recovering the cost of printing. The professor still hopes a publisher will reprint the book as he demonstrates its value in the classroom. It's rather common for professors to self-publish books for use in their classes, but most would prefer to be published by regular publishing houses and have their books promoted nationwide.

Generally, self-publishing is not a good alternative for a writer. Unless a market for the book is easily accessed, as in the cases described above, more often than not, self-published authors have a room in their home devoted to storing unsold books. Thousands of dollars later, many self-published authors discover there is more to publishing a book than just getting it printed. It's *after* the books are printed, stacked, and ready to hit the market that they realize they are in trouble. Most find that getting their words into print is less fulfilling than they had expected and that fame and fortune are elusive. Rarely does a self-published book bring the author recognition and prestige, although there are exceptions. Bernard Kamaroff wrote and published *Small-Time Operator* and has sold nearly 500,000 copies because he has a well-tuned marketing apparatus; and Ken Keyes writes personal growth books and has sold over 3 million copies, again as a result of an aggressive marketing plan. These isolated cases of success notwithstanding, there can be little doubt that publishing houses are better equipped than authors to oversee the production and promotion of books.

Promoting a book requires a marketing plan and contacts. Most self-publishers have no idea how to use a book's jacket to attract orders before publication, how to announce the book's publication to the world, or how to get the book distributed to bookstores throughout the country and abroad.

Bookstore purchasing agents buy almost exclusively from publishers or book distributors on established terms and under specific patterns of trade. They are regularly visited by book representatives who solicit orders, and they attend trade shows to learn of new books and place orders for them. Since people who are self-published don't know how to access these marketing routes, most of their books remain unsold, leaving them with unrecovered printing costs—and a little embarrassed, to boot. Still, there *are* ways to promote and sell self-published books, and these methods are discussed in Chapter 13.

Publishers are often approached by authors who have printed their own work. Many self-published authors believe their work has a better chance of being picked up by a commercial publisher after it has been printed, but just the opposite is true. Publishers are biased against self-published books because they know authors usually resort to self-publishing after they are unable to attract a commercial publisher. A self-published book is a signal that the manuscript has made the rounds of publishing houses and was rejected, and although the book is now nicely printed and bound, the same reasons for not publishing it are still relevant. On the other hand, a publisher doesn't know if an unprinted manuscript has been to many publishers and is more inclined to take an unbiased look at it.

As you can see, there are times when self-publishing is an appropriate way to get into print, but generally, this is not the case.

Subsidy Publishing and Vanity Presses

Subsidy publishing refers to books printed by publishing houses, but some or all of the cost of the publishing process, from editing to printing, is borne by the author. The publishers earn money by selling their services to writers. Subsidy publishers are also called "vanity presses" because they appeal to the ego or vanity of writers who want to see their work in print. A subsidy publisher is rarely the right choice if the book is designed for the general public because subsidy publishers spend little or no money promoting their publications since their main source of income is from authors who pay for the editing and printing process; they have little to gain from sales of the book. Without active promotion, a book can languish and never reach the market. On the other hand, some subsidy publishers ask the author for a percent of the publication costs, and the publisher pays the remainder. Thus, these publishers have money at risk, and this will cause them to spend more money and effort promoting the book.

Subsidy publishing is sometimes an acceptable method of getting a manuscript into print for the same reason self-publishing is sometimes acceptable; that is, if you write a manuscript with little commercial value but want the work published to provide copies to family or friends, or maybe to use as a special text in classes or as a working guide for employees. Women's organizations frequently raise money by gathering recipes for cookbooks and having them printed by subsidy publishers. They sell the books for more than the cost of printing, leaving a profit for their organization. A regular publisher wouldn't be interested in printing these types of books because of the limited number of potential buyers.

The advantage of using a subsidy publisher rather than self-publishing is that the subsidy publisher offers editorial services and has more experience in layout and book design. The book will probably look and read better if produced by a subsidy publisher rather than if it is self-published, but this service can be quite expensive. You must decide if you are willing to pay for the services offered by the subsidy publisher in order to have a better-produced book.

Before signing with a subsidy publisher, be sure to understand the contract, including how many books will be printed, the quality of the paper and material to be used, if any effort will be made to promote the book, and how much editorial work will be provided. In other words, you need to know what you will get for your money.

Even though the publishing house does not promote your book, you can still make money through self-promotion. (See Chapter 13 to learn how to get your book before the buying public.)

Book Packagers—What are They?

Book packagers, sometimes called book producers or book developers, create books. They organize whatever talent is needed to produce a book, including writers, photographers, artists, and editors, and can deliver a product ready for printing. They might find an author to write another person's story or idea, or team a ghostwriter with a celebrity. After the book is written, they then sell the package to a publisher.

The number of book packagers has increased significantly during the last decade. Many are also literary agents, and some of them have created best sellers. Book packagers have evolved, in part, because people have fascinating stories to tell but don't know how to write, and publishers want to print books on certain subjects but need the manuscripts written. The services of book packagers are especially attractive to book publishers with small staffs. The staff might start a project but turn it over to a book packager to complete. This frees the publishing staff to move on to other projects.

As a writer, you can sell your services to a packager who will team you with someone who has a story to tell that would be of commercial value—perhaps a celebrity, or someone who has "inside information." This is not a good way to become established as a writer because you work as a ghostwriter, receiving money for the work, but not the name recognition an author expects. It's a type of work-for-hire arrangement. Another payment schedule sometimes offered is a large advance but a low royalty percentage. If you are interested in working in this capacity, submit a well-crafted query with your writing résumé and a list of areas of expertise to book packagers or literary agents who also function as book packagers. A listing of book packagers is included in writers' directories.

Chapter 12

THE MECHANICS OF PREPARING AND SUBMITTING A BOOK MANUSCRIPT

You have two goals when preparing and submitting a book manuscript. The first is that the manuscript arrives at its destination in good condition; the second goal is that you appear to be a professional to the editor or agent who receives it. The manuscript you send should be prepared according to accepted industry standards, and the method of submission should ensure that the manuscript arrives safely in the hands of the most appropriate editor or agent.

Manuscript Format

A manuscript should be prepared the same way whether you are submitting it to a publisher or an agent. It should be printed on good quality 8 1/2 x 11 inch white paper, and double-spaced with a 1 to 1 1/4 inch margin on all sides. Single spacing is a glaring sign of inexperience. Even tables and sidebars should be double-spaced to allow the editor sufficient room for comments and corrections, but long quotes and footnotes can be single-spaced. The manuscript should be carefully proofread and should not contain crossouts or insertions. The top line of each page, other than the first page of each chapter, should consist of your name flushed left and the page number flushed right. Pagination should be continuous from the beginning to the end, not within chapters. Make sure the print is dark, and separate the pages and remove side strips when using continuous, tractor-fed computer paper.

The format is essentially the same as that used for article- and short-story manuscripts (see page 127). Start each chapter on a new page, and drop down about one-third of the page before beginning the chapter. When submitting poetry, type one poem per page. If the poems are longer than one page, clip together the pages of each poem.

Number the illustrations and photos, and indicate within the manuscript where each should be inserted. Place all illustrations and captions at the end of the written manuscript. Publishers who print color photos prefer 35mm color slides rather than color prints. Those who print b/w photos favor 8 x 10 inch glossy prints. Protect slides and negatives by inserting them in clear plastic covers, and protect photos from bending by placing them between thin cardboard sheets. Keep a copy of all photographs in case the ones you send are damaged or lost, and don't send original art work until you have a contract with a publisher. After the book has been produced, ask for the return of the originals; they will be needed for promotional articles.

Submitting a Manuscript

Place the printed pages and illustrations in a sturdy box (a typing or computer paper box is fine) and fill the empty space at the top and sides with bubble paper, foam sheets, or crumpled paper toweling. Don't use cardboard as filler as this would significantly increase the weight. Secure the box with shipping tape (not string) and write your name and address *on the box, along with the message "Return postage guaranteed."* Place the box in a shipping bag or wrap it in sturdy paper. Don't overwrap, overstaple, or overtape. Make sure your package is secure, but don't send something that will take a demolition team to open. You can write your return address and the address of the agent or publisher to whom it is being sent directly on the package, or you can use a mailing label for this information. Place clear tape over the addresses to ensure that they won't be smeared in the event the package gets wet.

Include either postage for the return of the manuscript or an SASE for a reply without the return of the manuscript. If sending postage for the manuscript's return, attach it to the cover letter with a paper clip, or include a large SASE that will accommodate the manuscript. Don't expect an agent or publisher to return a manuscript unless you provide adequate postage for its return. Many will keep manuscripts on file for a year or so and then discard them if postage is not provided. You may prefer to have only the photos and illustrations returned because the manuscript will get tattered while it is being read and shuffled between reviewers. It won't cost much more than return postage to make a new copy, and it's worth the extra cost to have a fresh copy to send to the next publisher or agent you solicit. For this reason, many writers send an SASE for a reply and the return of artwork and photos, but they make a new copy of the manuscript for the next submission.

Many writers prefer to send their manuscripts by United Postal Service (UPS) rather than the U.S. Postal Service, but they can't be sent UPS if the mailing address is a post office box number; they must have a street address. When the post office is used, most writers ship first class, but you can also send manuscripts by fourth class book rate. Fourth class book rate costs much less, but it may take a day or two longer for packages sent this way to arrive at their destination. With one exception, to be mentioned shortly, I have always shipped manuscripts by fourth class book rate, and they have always arrived at their destinations safely.

There are several ways for you to learn that your manuscript has reached its destination. The least expensive and most straightforward way is to include a self-addressed, stamped postcard and ask the editor or agent to return the card to you upon receiving the manuscript. The only problem with this method is the package may not be opened immediately, and you can spend sleepless nights wondering if your manuscript is lost. You can also be informed of the manuscript's arrival if it is sent Certified Mail or Registered Mail. Both services are offered by the U.S. Postal Service. Registered Mail, which costs about four times as much as Certified Mail, is the most secure method because the package must be signed in and out of each postal station en route while Certified Mail is only signed for when it reaches its destination. A confirmation of arrival receipt is available with each of these services. If you do not receive confirmation that the manuscript has arrived at its destination, call the publisher or agent to whom it was addressed, and if it has not been received, immediately contact the postal service to "put a trace on it." My first book manuscript (the only one I've sent by First Class mail) was lost en route but found through the tracing service.

Several months might elapse between the time you

send your manuscript and the time you either get it returned (and rejected) or receive word of acceptance and are offered a contract. During this time you will probably find all kinds of changes you'd like to make in the manuscript, but keep them to yourself until a contract is signed. Don't send minor revisions and ask the editor to insert them into the manuscript because, not only is this an imposition, but the changes might get lost or be inserted in the wrong places. After a manuscript has been sold, it is important to send a new copy of the complete manuscript that contains all revisions. Be sure to *ask that the old copy be destroyed.* This may seem like a trivial matter, but major problems can develop if you keep sending small changes that are incorrectly incorporated into the manuscript.

Keep accurate records of the date and to whom you send manuscripts. If, after several months, you don't hear from the editor or agent who received your manuscript, write or call to learn the status of the review. As you now realize, the process of locating a publisher or an agent can run into many months, even years, so make every effort to stay on top of the procedure in order to keep the process moving along.

You may worry that someone might steal your written work when you send proposals and manuscripts to so many places, but it is not necessary to register a manuscript at the copyright office in order to protect it. According to the 1978 Copyright Law, you become the owner of the work at the time it is created. If you are concerned about establishing ownership, mail yourself a registered copy of the complete manuscript. Don't open the package but keep it sealed in case you need to prove your authorship at a future date. Few writers bother to do this because it is exceedingly rare that an agent or publisher steals an author's work.

Chapter 13

PROMOTING YOUR BOOK

Plan to play an active role in promoting your book, both at the local and national levels.

Local and Hometown Media Coverage

"LOCAL WRITER MAKES GOOD"—can't you see that as a headline? Writers who have books published make good press in their local news media. In smaller communities it's easy to get coverage in both the printed press as well as on radio and television. Local writers become celebrities because of the amount of coverage they can garner. This leads to invitations to speak and book signing parties. It's amazing how many organizations are looking for speakers, and you can expect a flurry of invitations when your story hits the press. The easiest way to prepare for these lectures is to use one of the promotional articles, discussed below, as the text for your lecture. After a few presentations you will feel relaxed and will probably enjoy these outings. Always take along copies of your book to sell. You will be able to buy books from the publisher at around the wholesale price but can sell them at retail price, thus earning a tidy profit. (You should also receive some remuneration for these lectures.)

If you have moved, but still have contacts in your hometown (perhaps your friends or relatives still reside there), you can expect generous media attention in your hometown papers because a little distance does wonders for one's reputation. This makes going home for a visit an occasion for book signings and interviews. It's rather nice to be considered a "success" by old school chums who may wonder in amazement how this could come to pass.

While you should never pass up an invitation for an interview with the media, it's wise to create a touch of mystique by not revealing too much about your personal life. This will keep the public wanting more, and you and your books will remain subjects of interest.

When your book is about to be released, your publisher will send you a promotional questionnaire. You will be asked to list your local and hometown newspapers along with other outlets that might be appropriate for press releases that announce the publication of your book. This is an important marketing tool that can greatly increase the exposure of your book to the public. Completing the promotional questionnaire is your opportunity to inform the publisher of interest groups that may be curious about your book, and you can suggest methods of promotion. You should spend considerable time and thought on this questionnaire because the publisher's marketing department will be very receptive to outlets and promotional ideas you can offer but that they may have overlooked. Releases will be sent to the media outlets you list, and reporters may contact you for further development of their stories. If you would like a particular reporter to work on your story, be sure to indicate this in the promotional questionnaire, and the press release will be sent directly to that reporter.

Besides sending press releases, your publisher will send copies of your book to selected periodicals and newspapers in an effort to attract book reviews. The number of copies used for this purpose may run from just a few to several hundred.

Promoting Your Book Nationally

There are many ways to attract national attention. The best ways to reach the largest number of people are by writing articles for national magazines and appearing on national television and numerous radio shows.

Having your work appear in national magazines was discussed in Part I, but it is such an important and effective way to promote books, increase sales, and increase royalty payments, that it is being repeated here. From the discussion in Part II, it should be apparent that writers usually encounter considerable competition when they try to get articles published in magazines. Authors of books often circumvent that competition by gaining direct access to the decision makers who are looking for "authorities" to write for their publications. If you have authored a book, you are considered an authority. As soon as you complete writing your book manuscript and while it is being produced, start putting together articles on the same subject as your book. Don't try to sell the articles until it is about time for your book to be released. Write lots of articles! The articles need to differ somewhat from each other but always cover the central subject of your book. Always mention the book in the articles, and include a sidebar that identifies you as the author with a note that explains how and where it can be purchased. Editors are usually more than willing to include this information because it reinforces the message that their contributors are qualified to write the articles that appear in their publications. This type of promotion is a great way to generate income because it supports book sales and brings in revenue from articles. You can expect to be paid more for articles after you have had a book or two published.

Many thousands of magazines are published in the United States, and you can surely find a number of outlets for articles on the subject of your book, no matter how specialized or restricted the subject might be. Aggressively seek publication in these magazines if you want to increase the sale of your book.

Don't release all of the articles at once, but start with several and then keep them flowing through several years. Of course, by this time you will probably have another book under way and may want to put less energy into promotion—but keep up this activity as long as it is practical.

Talk shows are another productive way for newly published authors to promote their books. These appearances are usually arranged by the publisher, and the travel costs to the show's place of origin may be split between the publisher and the show's producer, although there are many variations for these arrangements.

There was a time when publishers built large advertising budgets into the cost of promoting a book. During this period they supported author tours, arranged television appearances, underwrote book-signing parties, and placed advertisements in a variety of media in an effort to create interest in the book. Now, with tight budgets and the need for cost-effective promotion, publishers are reluctant to underwrite the whirlwind author's tour except to promote new publications by their big-name writers. The trend is toward television appearances for big-name writers and radio interviews for less well-known ones. Television satellite hookups are quite expensive and are done only for important interviews, but radio interviews are very inexpensive, costing only the charge of a phone call.

Since publisher-sponsored promotional tours are rare, it's worth doing what YOU can to help promote your book. When traveling, inform your publisher of your itinerary. They may take advantage of your travels by setting up interviews with the media and promoting book-signing events in the larger cities you plan to visit. If your publisher is not interested in this type of promotion, you can set up these events yourself. Remember, promoting book sales is in your best interest, so if your publisher doesn't aggressively push your book, it's up to you to get it before the public. When you know you will be visiting a city, send a press release to the local media, and, if you can get a story, ask the larger bookstores if they would be interested in a book-signing party, since it will get free publicity from the press story. You will be surprised at how much action you can get just by asking.

Talk shows that are useful in promoting a book are the long-distance phone interviews and call-in programs for radio. I prefer these to on-site shows and often do them because they take no more time than a phone conversation from my home office. They are arranged by the publisher's marketing department, or you can set them up yourself if you are promoting a self-published book. Simply send notices of your book's publication, along with letters ask-

ing for an interview, to the program directors of radio stations across the country. You can find the addresses of
radio stations (and newspapers that might be interested in
interviews) listed in *Gale Directory of Publications and
Broadcast Media* (see page 259). This publication indicates
the power, and thus the coverage, of each radio station and
the circulation of each newspaper. Obviously, you should
direct your energy to the outlets that will provide the greatest exposure.

As you continue to write and talk about a subject, your
confidence will be bolstered, and you will become increasingly comfortable with the topic. I've seen authors build
whole careers around a single subject, starting with a book,
then articles, columns, lectures, and talk shows. Then they
write another book and the cycle starts all over again.

Promoting Self-Published Books

Bookstores are more inclined to stock books published
by regular publishing houses, and people are more inclined
to purchase books published by regular publishing houses
than books that are self-published. For this reason, use a
name for your publishing company that doesn't "spill the
beans." If your name is Bob Jones, don't use the name Bob
Jones or BJ Publishing Company. Instead, use a publishing
name that alludes to the types of books you write but does
not include a hint of your own name.

Some of the methods used to promote books printed by commercial publishers can also be used to promote self-published books; it's just that you must do all the legwork, send out press releases, and set up interviews. Talk show hosts rarely invite authors of self-published books to appear on their shows, so your best bet at attracting a large audience is to write numerous articles for national magazines. This will allow you to keep a presence within your target market.

Self-published books are frequently sold through mail order, so it's necessary to inform potential customers of your product. You might want to try a few strategically-placed advertisements. These will only be cost-effective if you can target a very defined market. For instance, the person who self-published a book for people wanting to start small businesses had natural outlets in magazines like *Small Business Opportunities* or *New Business Opportunities*. Both are directed specifically to people with small business interests. A herbalist who writes about holistic medicine might advertise in *Preventive Medicine*. Even small advertisements can be quite costly, so use your writing skills to make every word count, and write an ad that will hook the readers and inspire them to order your book.

Another way to sell by mail order is to use direct mail, sending letters or flyers to people who have indicated through previous purchases that they may have an interest in the book. For instance, this book might be promoted by sending flyers to people who subscribe to *The Writer* or *Writer's Digest*, both of which are monthly trade magazines that deal with the writing and publishing business. Mailing lists can be purchased from companies that specialize in compiling lists of people with special interests. Look in the telephone directories of medium to large cities under "Mailing Lists" to locate companies that sell these lists.

If you find yourself doing a lot of mail-order selling, it would probably be a good idea to rent a postal box. A post office box number looks more professional than a home address, especially if you live on a street that sounds very neighborhood-like, such as Shady Lane. A post office box will also help you keep a low profile in the neighborhood, and neighbors will remain oblivious to your second career as writer-publisher. A post office box number also puts space between you and your customers, and this is desirable because the really curious might be inclined to drop in rather than communicate by mail if they know your home address.

As you can see, writers can contribute to their own success through creative promotion. Writer-philosopher Wilson Mizner might have been referring to these authors when he wrote, "The gent who wakes up and finds himself a success hasn't been asleep."

PART IV

STRATEGIES FOR SUCCESS

Chapter 14

YOUR WRITING BUSINESS

The first three parts of this book were designed to serve as guides to help you convert your manuscripts into printed books and articles. This fourth part deals with strategies for success that will enhance your writing career and increase the probability that you will become a successful writer.

The way you think about your writing career will influence your success as a writer. Some of you think of writing as a hobby—something to be done in your spare time—while others of you approach writing as a business venture and bring to it a shrewd business sense. Whether you intend to earn a bundle or barely enough to cover the cost of manuscript paper and postage, you will take your work more seriously and be more productive if you think of your writing efforts as a business venture. Also, functioning as a business offers many advantages to writers who work at home. This chapter will explain some of the reasons it is wise to organize your writing as a business with you functioning as a sole proprietor.

A sole proprietorship is a business owned and operated by one person who is responsible for its debts and losses and assumes all its risks. At least 85 percent of the home businesses in America are organized in this manner, which means, essentially, that the owner is self-employed.

It is easy to start a sole proprietorship. There are no special forms of organization or legal documents required; the owner starts the business by hanging out a shingle and getting to work and stops the business by failing to show up for work. Also, there is little governmental control. In fact, the government encourages this type of business by allowing business losses to be deducted from the owner's other earned income before taxes are figured. As you will learn, this tax advantage can significantly reduce the tax burden of writers who organize their writing activities as a home business.

Strive to Create a Business Image

You will be known, not by how you look at business meetings, but by how you look on paper. In most instances, editors will only know you and your work through letters and manuscripts, and your only opportunity to create a business image will be based on these communications.

It's worth spending a little time and money creating the image you wish to project. You need a business name, and you might want to design a logo to go with it. Have stationery printed on good quality paper, using your business name and logo in the letterhead. Since most writers don't bother to have stationery printed, you will immediately set your work apart from the crowd by looking better on paper. Besides stationery, you should also have a supply of business cards printed. Attaching one to each query letter or cover letter, with a hand-written note on the card about the subjects you cover, can lead to assignments. Design the card so there is space to write, and have them printed on flat, rather than glossy, card stock so the ink from your hand-written message will not smear. Your calling cards should match your stationery with the same color and style.

The cost of printing letterhead and calling cards is determined by the number printed, with the cost per sheet or card decreasing as the number of copies printed increases. While you don't want to spend too much as you establish your business, you will save money in the long run if you have at least 500 sheets of stationery, matching business-size envelopes, and calling cards printed. Ask the printer for the originals when the job is completed so you will have them for subsequent printings. With stationery and calling cards prepared, you are ready to approach editors and publishers with queries, proposals, and manuscripts that will convey a professional image.

On some occasions, editors, publishers, or agents will phone in response to something you have sent them. You don't want to miss these calls, so if you work during the day or are away from the phone for long periods, it's worth buying a telephone answering machine. Be sure the recorded message you leave on the machine sounds professional and appropriate, and return the calls received on your answering machine as soon as possible. By the way, you don't need to tell editors whether you write full time or only after working all day at another job. Unless they ask, let them assume you are a full-time writer.

Business Taxes

The tax advantage of working at home is one good reason to organize your writing as a business. Even if you work a regular job and write only part time and earn very little or no money through your writing, it is in your best interest to organize your writing efforts as a business to take advantage of tax breaks offered to workers with home offices.

The following explanation about how to qualify for

business deductions is rather detailed and lengthy, but it is important for you to understand the many types of business taxes and learn how to take advantage of tax breaks because these can literally make your writing business pay for itself. By taking advantage of tax breaks, you can offset earnings from other sources with expenses associated with your writing business, and this can result in a larger net profit, even if you are unable to sell many of your manuscripts.

Although the government takes a portion of your earnings, you are allowed a considerable number of tax deductions. Your goal is to operate in such a way that taxes can be reduced to as low a level as permitted by law. The government expects as much and has written the laws realizing that this is the prerogative and goal of each taxpayer. If you work at home, like most writers, *and have established your writing as a business rather than a hobby,* you can take deductions for a portion of home maintenance and improvements, telephone expenses, office and work space, major purchases related to your work, and a host of other items. All of these deductions can be claimed even if you work at another job and write only in the evening or on weekends.

An awareness of how to use the tax structure to your advantage will influence how you set up your work space, keep records, and engage in business activities; the sooner you learn the regulations, the more money you will save. But keep in mind that tax laws change. Therefore, use this chapter as a guide, but consult current references or an accountant who can advise you regarding changes in the tax code.

The IRS Asks, "Is it a Hobby or a Business?"

Business is defined as an activity engaged in for profit while a hobby is an activity engaged in for pleasure. Most writers work at home, and their work may look more like a hobby than a business. It is important to clearly define your writing as a business venture because the IRS is watching for people who take business deductions for hobby expenses.

It's common knowledge that if you make money selling manuscripts, even though you consider your writing to be a hobby instead of a business, you are expected to pay taxes on the income. You can deduct the expenses associated with the hobby from the earnings to arrive at your taxable income. However, if you lose money at your hobby as a result of spending more on supplies and equipment than you take in, you are not entitled to a deduction greater than the income derived from the hobby. If you pursue the same hobby, organize it as a business for the purpose of earning a profit, but lose money instead, then you can deduct ALL of the expenses of your writing business and offset the loss against other income.

The question is, "When does an activity cease to be a hobby and become a business?" There is confusion about this question because some taxpayers do not understand the ruling that states "if an activity makes a profit in three out of five years it is presumed NOT to be a hobby" (IRS Publication 525). They interpret this to mean that, if an activity LOSES money in three out of five years, it is considered to be a hobby, but that is not the case. The question to be considered is, "Is the activity engaged in for profit?" If the answer is yes, even though it fails to make a profit, it is considered to be a business. The IRS has ways of evaluating activities to determine if there is a profit-making motive, but there is no set standard; each case is decided on its own merits. If the profit motive is evident, then the business can lose money for many years and the expenses can be deducted from other income. One case (#68TC696), taken to court, ruled in favor of an artist who strived for twenty years to earn a profit but continued to operate at a loss. The artist's expenses were allowed as business deductions because she successfully demonstrated that her goal was to generate income and earn a profit (she took classes, entered art shows, etc).

The following procedures will help convince the IRS you are engaged in a business to earn a profit:

1. Your work is conducted in a businesslike manner, and appropriate records are maintained.

2. A reasonable amount of time and effort is spent trying to be successful; i.e., earn a profit.

3. You are a skilled writer and at least occasionally get into print and are paid for your work.

4. Your financial status doesn't suggest you are looking for a tax write-off, but you are trying to earn some income.

5. You spend money for equipment, stationery, and the other trappings of a business.

Be sure to use Schedule C to report your writing income and expenses. The very fact that Schedule C is used indicates that you intend to engage in a business for profit. Hobby income is reported on Form 1040, line 22 under "Other Income," and allowable hobby expenses are reported on Schedule A under miscellaneous deductions.

Kinds of Taxes

You are required to pay taxes on the money you earn as a writer, including royalties you receive from the sale of books, income from articles, short stories and poetry, and fees you receive for readings and lectures. You are not required to pay taxes on prize money if the award was granted for past performance and not in expectation of services to be performed.

You are also required to pay taxes on earnings received from publications in foreign countries, but you can avoid double taxation (paying to both the foreign and U.S. governments) by completing a form, available from your foreign publisher. The completion and filing of this form will exempt you from foreign taxation.

You will be required to pay taxes to both the federal and state governments when you earn money as a writer. The next section explains the federal taxes you are obligated to pay and briefly explains the most common type of state taxes, although you will need to learn if they apply in the area where you live.

Federal Taxes

The kinds of federal taxes that apply to freelance writers, working as sole proprietors, and the tax forms that are used to figure and submit them are listed below. These can be used by full-time writers as well as those who work at another job but spend evenings or weekends preparing manuscripts with the goal to be published and earn a profit. The tax forms can be obtained from your district IRS office or by writing the U.S. Government Printing Office, Superintendent of Documents, Washington, D.C. 20402, or by calling the IRS 800 number listed in the Blue Pages of your telephone directory under "United States Government, IRS Forms."

The federal tax forms you will need include:

- 1040   Individual Income Tax Return. If you and/or your spouse are earning money from another job, you will already use this form to report income.

- 1040C   Profit or Loss from Business or Profession. This form is used to itemize business deductions, and using it is a clear indication to the IRS that you consider yourself to be in business, even though you may be making very little money or operating at a loss.

- 1040ES Estimated Tax for Individuals, paid quarterly. Taxes are withheld throughout the year from the wages earned by people working for someone else. But, as a self-employed individual, you are responsible for making periodic payments of your estimated federal income tax. It is very difficult for writers to estimate taxes because of the "feast-or-famine" nature of the business. Still, estimated tax payments are due by the 15th of January, April, June, and September. It is usually safe to pay taxes on what you have already brought in, unless you find yourself making huge amounts of money from your writing, which is very rare. If you receive a large amount of unexpected money—perhaps an advance on a book—just increase your estimated tax at the next payment time. You must pay at least 90 percent of the taxes owed, or you will be penalized. Estimated tax payment forms are available from the IRS.

- 1040SE   Computation of Social Security Self-Employment Tax. Your estimated tax payments will also include payment into your Social Security fund (known as FICA). All self-employed people must file a Self-Employment Form when the profit claimed on Schedule C reaches $600. At this point the self-employed person starts paying into a personal Social Security account at a rate specified by the government. Your payment of the self-employment tax contributes to your coverage under the social security system, which provides you with future retirement benefits and medical insurance benefits (Medicare).

- Form 8829. Used to claim Home-Use deductions. See pages 231-235.

State and Local Taxes

Taxes vary among states but most have an income tax. This tax is calculated on net income and is usually due at the same time federal tax returns are filed. Some cities also levy taxes on income, so it is important to check with your city income tax bureaus to see if this applies to you. If you must pay state and local taxes, they are deductible as a business expense and should be listed on Schedule C of your federal tax form.

Business Deductibles

Federal taxes are paid on net income. Net income is determined by deducting expenses and allowable deductions from gross income. Business deductions are allowed for expenses incurred in the course of doing business. A writer can claim the cost of the following items and activities as tax-deductible expenses. Study the list of the kinds of expenses you can deduct from your gross income as you compute the net income on which taxes will be calculated.

Allowable Business Deductions

Agent's fees and commissions
Books and manuals dealing with writing
Briefcase
Delivery charges
Dues to professional organizations
Education expenses for writing and marketing seminars and workshops
Equipment lease costs (computer, copying, and fax machines, etc.)
Labor costs for independent contractors (typist, researcher)
Legal fees
Marketing references

Office equipment
Office furniture
Office supplies
Tape recorder (for interviews)
Photo equipment, supplies, and printing
Post office box rental
Postage
Printing
Promotional expenses
Publisher solicitation expenses
Research expenses
Stationery, business cards
Subscriptions to periodicals and journals
Travel expenses related to writing or research
Writers' conferences fees and expenses

Home-Use Deductions

One way to save money by writing at home is by taking advantage of the tax deductions allowed for home work space. By learning what is required to make work space tax deductible, you can plan your space to fulfill the requirements. This effort is worthwhile because these deductions can amount to a significant savings. The items that are tax deductible include a percent of the utility expenses, mortgage interest, insurance, maintenance and repair costs, and the total amount of money spent developing the area used for your writing business.

To qualify for a deduction, the part of the home used for your writing business must meet certain qualifications. It must be:

1. Clearly *separated* from family living space

2. Used *exclusively* for your writing business

3. Used on a *regular* basis, and

4. Be your *principal* place of business

A *freestanding structure* used exclusively and regularly for business purposes also qualifies. Each of these requirements is explained below.

1. Separation from family space: The easiest way to separate your writing area from family space is to confine it to a room behind a door or in a separate building, but that isn't always practical or possible. Separation can also be accomplished through the use of screens, partitions, and furniture arrangement. A desk used only for writing, but placed within a room used by the family will not meet the "separation" requirement.

2. Exclusive use: Exclusive use means the designated area is used only for your writing activities, which includes writing, reading, interviewing, and doing research. For example, if your spouse takes the family car from the garage each morning and drives to work, and you set up a work station in the area where the car had been, you cannot claim the deduction because the garage is not used exclusively for business purposes. If, however, the car is parked outside of the garage and you leave your work station permanently set up, this would meet the exclusive use provision.

3. Regular use:　Regular use means the business part of your home is used on a regular and continuing basis. It does not need to be used each day, but regularly, such as three times a week or every weekend. Even if a part of a home is used exclusively for writing, but it is used only occasionally, it does not meet the requirement and cannot be claimed as a deduction.

4. Principal place of business:　The part of a home claimed for a business deduction must be the principal place of business. If you work outside of your home during the day but work on manuscripts at home in the evenings or on weekends, then your home workspace would be the principal place of business for your writing business and would qualify for a deduction.

Freestanding structures:　A separate, freestanding structure is tax deductible if the structure is used *exclusively* and *regularly* for business purposes; it does not need to be the principal place of business. A freestanding structure could be a trailer, shop, studio, barn, chicken coop, garage, or the like. In other words, even though you claim an office inside your home but also use a trailer or other structure for a study zone where you read and plan projects, you can claim the second structure as a tax-deductible zone if that is the sole purpose of the structure.

The amount of deduction allowed for the business use of your home is based on the percent of the home used for business purposes. The percentage can be figured in either of two ways. The preferred method is to divide the square feet in the home by the number of square feet used for business purposes. Thus, if, in a 3000 square foot home, 500 square feet are converted to business use, then 16.6 percent of home expenses can be claimed as a tax deduction. The other method for figuring space is to count the number of rooms (if they are nearly equal in size), and divide the number of rooms used for business purposes by the total number of rooms. If one room is used in a five-room house, then 1/5th or 20 percent of the home expenses are legitimate home-use business deductions. By the way, don't include the bathroom in the room count.

Calculate the amount of deductions attributable to business use by multiplying the total home expenses (utilities, repair, mortgage—see list) by the percent of space used in your business. For example, if it costs $5000 for total home expenses, and 10 percent of the home is used for business purposes, you can deduct $500 for the business use of your home. You can also deduct the complete cost of decorating, painting, or remodeling the business portion of the home.

For many years, the tax code read that the amount of deduction allowed for home use in a given year could not exceed the gross income the home business generated. However, starting in 1988, an important change was made and now home-use expenses greater than the gross income produced by a business *can be carried forward to the next year or years* until the gross income is large enough to deduct the entire amount. This change has proven to be especially helpful to beginning writers, many of whom struggle for years before they start to earn a profit. This change also helps established writers who have both profitable and lean periods.

It is advisable to enclose a photograph or two of your home office and work area with your tax return so the examiner can more fully understand how you are using the space you are claiming as a deduction. This type of documentation goes a long way toward warding off an audit.

Home-Use Tax-Deductible Expenses

A percent of the following expenses can be deducted from income before calculating taxes owed. The percent is based on the amount of your home floor space that is used for your writing business (see page 234.)

Rent

Mortgage interest

Insurance premiums on home

Utilities including gas, electricity, and water

Home repairs and maintenance including labor
and supplies

Cleaning and lawn care services and supplies

The total cost of decorating or remodeling the part of the home used for business purposes is tax-deductible. Also, the cost of all long-distance business calls and charges for extra business-related telephone services are tax-deductible.

Use tax form 8829 to claim these deductions. Using this form is an accurate way to calculate home-use expenses and serves as a convenient check list to make sure you claim all the deductions to which you are entitled.

Business-Related Travel Expenses

Travel to promote your writing career, whether it is to writers' conferences or to gather material for articles or books, is tax-deductible. That is true if the travel is by air, rail, bus, or personal automobile. To document your travel you should save ticket stubs, cancelled checks, and receipts. Travel by car cannot be documented so easily.

Writers don't usually log many miles in the pursuit of

their careers, and it is easier to use the standard mileage-rate deduction for those miles that qualify as tax deductible rather than keep track of the numerous expenses associated with owning a car and deducting a percent of the costs. Records are needed to determine how much deduction to claim. The records should show the business miles you drive during the year, and the easiest way to collect that information is to keep a record book in your car and record the date, mileage, and destination each time your outing is business related. Be prepared to present the log book if your expenses are questioned.

As you can see, the many tax deductions you can claim make it worthwhile to organize your writing as a business and to keep appropriate records.

Record Keeping

Keeping records for a writing business is simple and straightforward. The purpose of maintaining records is to track the history of your marketing efforts for each manuscript you write, ensure that payment is received for each manuscript sold, evaluate the progress of your writing career, and satisfy the requirements of the IRS. The same records used for business purposes are adequate for tax purposes.

The records you must maintain include:

1. A list of publishers or agents where each manuscript has been submitted, when and to whom each has been sold, and when payment is received.

2. A schedule of when royalty payments for each book in print is due and a notation when each is received.

3. Expenses associated with your writing business, to be used for tax documentation.

4. An account of payments received.

Each of these four types of records will now be discussed in detail.

Maintain marketing, sales and payment records for manuscripts for periodicals: The easiest way to keep track of manuscripts sent to different periodical publishers is to maintain a notebook with a chart for each manuscript. This chart was explained in Part II, Chapter 7 and indicates when and where each manuscript was submitted, if it was rejected or purchased, when it was published, and the amount paid for the article. After a manuscript has been purchased and you have received payment, the chart for that manuscript should be placed at the back of the folder and referred to when you attempt to resell the article.

Selling manuscripts to periodicals that pay on publication is not as desirable as selling to those that pay on acceptance, but you may resort to these outlets if you have trouble placing your work elsewhere. Make sure you are paid for your work. When a manuscript is accepted, ask when it will be published and make a notation in your calendar. If payment is not received one month after the publication date, write to inquire about the status of the article and the fee that is owed you.

Maintain marketing and sales records for book manuscripts: A record should be maintained that shows when and to whom you submit book queries and manuscripts. Follow the same procedure described for recording the marketing and sales of article manuscripts (Chapter 7). After a book contract is signed, start a file for all communications with your editor and publisher, including a copy of your contract, royalty statements, and check stubs. This file can become quite robust as your book is being produced and after it is on the market.

Record royalty payments: It is necessary to keep track of royalty payments if you have books in print. Book contracts specify when royalty payments are due, but customarily they are paid twice each year. Since payment is made so infrequently, it's easy to forget that something is owed to you. Make a note in your calendar when each payment is due. Some publishers pay promptly, but others require a little urging. Wait no longer than one month past the due date, then send a letter to the publisher stating you have not received your royalty payment. The late payers often send a note that the payment was overlooked. If you believe that, I've got some property in the Pacific to sell you! It may be closer to the truth that many small publishers operate on a very thin margin between being broke and just about being broke. If the publisher is still solvent, you will probably get your money.

I'm convinced many writers simply forget about royalty payments as they become preoccupied with other interests, and their publishers are hoping to get by without sending the money. Or, the longer the publisher can avoid paying, the longer they can use the money for other purposes. It's up to you to make sure payments are received. Of course, if you have an agent, payments will be closely monitored because the agent only gets his or her commission when the publisher sends the royalty payment. But then, you must keep alert and make sure the agent forwards your share to you.

Expense records: All expense records should be kept for tax purposes. These records are necessary to help you prepare tax returns without undue anxiety, and they may be needed in the event you are audited and need substantiation to verify your claims. Some receipts will be for out-of-pocket purchases, and it is helpful to note on the back of each receipt what was purchased. Stash the receipts in a large manila envelope, using a different envelope for each month or two, and noting the total amount on the outside.

Income records: Deposit all income from your writing business into a checking account, making a note of the income source. Your checking account can be used for income verification in the event of an IRS audit.

Each year, start a new "Income Received" list. While you will note when payment is received for each manuscript or royalty, it is wise to keep a running account of total receipts so you will know at any time your total earnings for the year in progress. With this information you will know how your business is progressing and be able to compare your successes from one year to another. This record also makes it easy to complete your tax forms and allows you to know immediately how much money you need to remit if you must pay estimated quarterly taxes.

Do You Need a Separate Bank Account?

As the year progresses, your checkbook will reflect many business transactions, and this valuable record will be needed to document income received and tax-deductible expenditures. A separate bank account is recommended for most home businesses because this allows the entrepreneur to clearly separate business expenses and income from personal expenses and income. Also, the IRS recognizes separate accounts as evidence of a business venture, and this is a good way to keep records for tax purposes. Nonetheless, you can probably forego the expense and trouble of a separate account for your writing business. This type of business has relatively few expenses, and payments for articles and royalties are easily identified as they are deposited. However, if you do not have a separate bank account, you should make every effort to keep exceptionally good records that can hold up under the scrutiny of an IRS audit.

Record Keeping Also Means Keeping Records.

As your writing business develops, contracts will accumulate, and it is important to safeguard them because they are as good as money in the bank. Keep contracts for books in a home safe or in a safe-deposit box at your bank. Book contracts are a part of your estate, just as surely as the deed to your home or stock certificates, and your heirs should be aware of the contracts and know where they are kept.

Some of your most valuable records are your inventory, and they must be protected. Inventory is considered in business circles to be every tangible item used in the pursuit of business. It includes products on hand that are for sale, raw materials that will be used to make products for sale, or parts used in repair work. Another term for inventory is "stock."

As a writer, you also need to build an inventory, but, unlike other businesses, you don't pay taxes on your stock because it is nothing more than the manuscripts in your desk or recorded on disks, and the photos, notes, and interviews that are the raw material you have gathered, ready to be turned into manuscripts. You should keep this type of material—your inventory—in a secure place, safe from theft or fire. It must be safeguarded as this is the product of your labor and a source of future income.

As your writing career develops, your inventory of manuscripts will grow, and eventually you could spend all your time marketing old articles, stories, or poems, but that is not recommended if you intend to grow as a writer. Still, using your inventory of manuscripts is a good way to keep articles in press and in the marketing pipeline while you are working on fresh material.

As you can see, keeping records and record keeping are essential if your business is to operate smoothly.

Chapter 15

MANAGING YOURSELF

Managing yourself is essential if you are to compete successfully in the writing business. You must learn to balance your professional and personal life, control your work schedule, manage your time and energy, and establish good work habits. As you strive to establish good work habits, also take your personal habits into consideration. Good habits can give you a sense of well-being and make the difference between feeling energetic and serene or tired and stressed out. Stand tall, hang loose, laugh easily, and take care of yourself. Practice moderation.

Managing Your Time

Our literature and lives are filled with expressions and

quotes about time. We have all heard the clichés "time marches on," and "time waits for no man." Quotes that come to mind include Benjamin Franklin's "Do not squander time, for that is the stuff life is made of," and Aristotle's "Time is the most valuable thing that a man can spend."

How much time do you have "on your hands?" Isn't that a strange expression? Every moment of every day is probably filled, so where do you expect to find enough time to write manuscripts and market them?

Time and energy are your most valuable resources and must be carefully spent. You have no choice but to spend your time, but try to spend it wisely. Learn to manage your time and consciously incorporate time-management procedures into your writing schedule and workday. Just being aware of the concept of time management will make you sensitive to lost moments and alert you to time bargains.

Getting More for Your Time and Energy

One of the first things you will discover as your writing business gets under way is that you don't have enough time or energy to do everything you would like. Recognize your time and energy limitations and discard some of your past roles as you acquire new ones. You will need to make choices and set priorities. If you have made the decision to devote time and energy to develop a writing career, you also need to make decisions about eliminating some of your other activities.

You must balance the things you want to do with the things you need to do in order to be successful. The quality of your life and the success of your writing career will depend upon how successfully you master this delicate balance.

Look for ways to save time. Routines and timesaving devices will help you get more done in less time. For instance, a postal scale can save the time it takes to go to the post office, a thesaurus and a dictionary incorporated into your computer word-processing program, a facsimile machine, and a fast printer can all save valuable time. Make an effort to keep apprised of new products that are designed to help you trim moments from your daily work.

We have a tendency to think other people waste our time but fail to recognize that we may be our own worst "time wasters." Determine when you are not using your time well by keeping a record of how you spend your day. Eliminate time-wasting activities such as reading junk mail, writing a letter when a telephone call would suffice, overextending a coffee or lunch break, or delaying decisions on unimportant matters. And practice saying "no."

Procrastination is a huge time waster. When a difficult passage seems to be looming before you, tackle it immediately. If you are intimidated by a section in your manuscript and not quite sure how to handle it, get some words down quickly because the perceived difficulty can cause you to become overwhelmed with anxiety, which can lead to writer's block. If you are attacked with writer's block, keep writing, even if you are only writing letters or writing in a diary.

Working at a job consistently is one of the secrets to getting a large quantity of work done. This powerful tactic has eluded many who find themselves swamped with too much to do. The secret to getting a manuscript completed is to work at it consistently, on a schedule, chipping away at it one word or one chapter at a time. To the old Latin proverb, "Make haste slowly" we might add, "but consistently."

Schedules Keep You Focused

Work must be focused if it is to be productive. Henry David Thoreau wrote, "It's not enough to be busy; so are the ants. The question is: What are we busy about?" The best way to keep focused and on track is to work from a schedule. To be functional, this schedule should be written down because only then can you compare the various jobs that need to be done and rank them in their order of importance.

You might find it useful to write your schedule in a

daily appointment book—the type that has a full page for each day. Start each day by checking your schedule and listing all the jobs you hope to accomplish. Next, prioritize the items on the list. Number the events, research, and writing tasks in their order of importance, and, starting with number one, work through the list. If your workday ends before the list is completed, transfer the unfinished tasks to the next day's schedule.

Your schedule book will become an excellent source of information. It will tell you when you did what. You might be surprised at how frequently you will refer to it to refresh your memory about past activities. It is in this book that you should note when royalty payments are due, when you should contact an editor or publisher about a manuscript, and so forth.

There is one other factor to consider as you prepare your daily schedule and that is *prime time*. This is your most productive part of the day. Try to identify your prime time and arrange your work schedule to take advantage of it by undertaking your most difficult tasks, such as starting a new chapter, during this time period. Also, it's helpful to end each day with a new chapter under way or something started so you don't have to fight an empty screen or page the first thing in the morning. With a new section started, it's much easier to get the juices flowing when you get back to work.

Controlling Interruptions

If you want to control your work day and save precious time, learn to control interruptions. Interruptions are a normal, yet time-consuming part of life, but, as you strive to make your writing business successful, you will need to flex your will and regulate intrusions into your time.

Interruptions will arrive with the ring of your door bell, the ring of your telephone, and with the delivery of your mail. Interruptions via the telephone or the front door are usually the most difficult to deal with. Your friends and family probably won't intentionally intrude upon your time, but it is up to you to establish your work hours, and make sure they are known to those who expect to share your life.

Make your telephone work for you rather than against you. The calls you make can save time, but the calls you receive can be time-consuming. Be prepared to deal with the other end of the line and learn to control the length of your conversations so you can get back to writing.

Juggling your writing career, family, friends, and other responsibilities requires dexterity. Sometimes the expectations of your family and friends will be different from those you have for yourself, and the question you must resolve is, "Whose goals and expectations will I fulfill?"

When your family and friends realize how serious you are about writing, they will respect the time you must devote to it, and they will be less inclined to ask you to plan the family reunion, help at the church banquet, and attend the endless array of other activities our society has deemed normal behavior but which interfere with doing the things we want to do. Writers want to write and can only be successful when given the time and space to work at their craft.

Besides interruptions from friends and family, you will be surprised at the number of requests that will come your way as you have successes in the publishing world. You will be asked to give talks, chair campaigns, be on public-service committees, and so forth. Of course, you may want to do some of these things, but you must be very selective about participating in conflicting activities if your writing career is to flourish and you are to produce a significant volume of work. It's not only that these activities take time from your work, but the break in your thoughts and in your daily routine can thwart your writing projects.

Requests are easier to handle if they arrive through the mail because you will have time to think about ways to respond. In any case, keep in mind that your time and energy are your most valuable resources, and learn to deal with interruptions quickly and efficiently so you can get on with the business of writing.

Surviving Dry Spells

The sharpest freelancer and the most aggressive writer-business person will hit dry spells when nothing sells. This happens both to beginning writers and to those who have been in the writing business for many years. You can expect this to happen, and plan for the weeks when nothing you do seems to be good enough and you can't attract a buyer.

The best way to survive dry spells is to keep writing and submitting your material to editors. However, you must consider the possibility that the reason you are having dry spells is your manuscripts are poorly written or your subject matter is inappropriate. If a manuscript is rejected after repeated attempts to sell it, take a fresh look at the work. Does the manuscript have a defined focus and address a specific audience? Is it well-crafted, and is the manuscript neat and presented in a professional manner? If you can answer "yes" to each of these questions, then why isn't the work selling? Maybe you aren't sending it to the right outlets, or maybe the manuscript isn't as good as you think it is. It might be wise to ask a friend or colleague to look at the work for an outside opinion. If you conclude that the manuscript is well-written and is on a subject of interest, then it's just a matter of keeping up the marketing effort until your manuscript is matched with the right editor.

During these dry spells, you might work on your

inventory of ideas. The value of building an inventory of manuscripts was discussed in the last chapter. You should also build an inventory of ideas as you go about your daily work. We sometimes think successful writers are like hermits, locked away in remote attics and slaving away over their manuscripts, but just the opposite is true. While quiet time and isolation are needed, a writer must have experiences in order to write with conviction and passion. These experiences are rarely acquired in isolation. Ralph Waldo Emerson wrote, "Talent alone cannot make a writer. There must be a man behind the book." Your life and experiences are your greatest source of ideas. Cultivate relationships that enable you to live life fully. Read and explore ideas and feelings because these will be the backbone of your work. A backlog of ideas is valuable to writers, and it is wise to keep a notebook handy and record ideas and experiences. Another way to build an inventory of ideas is to write a daily diary of your thoughts and observations.

The Value of Networking, Conferences, and Writers' Guilds

There is value in gathering with other writers. Writers can learn from each other by sharing experiences, and they offer each other emotional and intellectual support. There are two main types of settings where writers gather. The first is conferences and the other is writers' groups or guilds.

Writers' conferences are listed in the May issue of *The Writer* and in *Literary Market Place,* among other places. There are many conferences held throughout the year, with at least one in nearly every region of the country. Most conferences do not have admission requirements. They are good places to make contact with agents and network with other writers. Often, it is the unscheduled gathering or the talk over coffee where writers learn of what and how other writers are doing. These contacts and tips sometimes prove to be invaluable and can lead writers to agents or editors who are interested in their material. Writers' conferences are also valuable because they are a source of inspiration, and most writers leave a conference pumped up, ready to take on another project or with the courage to complete the one in progress, along with ideas about marketing their work.

Some conferences are not open to all applicants. The organizers of restricted conferences screen applicants and limit enrollment to very talented, although not necessarily widely published, writers.

Agents go to writers' conferences looking for new talent. If you attend a conference and become acquainted with an agent who handles the kind of material you write, and if you have a little chemistry between you (it helps if you like and respect your agent), then you might mention you are looking for an agent to represent you. Ask if you can send some of your work for reading and possible representation. Be sure to ask for a business card so you send your manuscript to the correct name and address! If you don't have anything ready to submit, then write a brief letter about one week after your encounter to restate your background and writing interest, and thank the agent for taking the time to talk with you. By writing this letter you are preparing for the day when your work is ready to be submitted.

Writers' groups and guilds are also valuable sources of information and support. Look for one in your community, and if none is organized, find a few other writers to meet with regularly to exchange ideas, tips, and information.

There are scores of writers' organizations around the country. For a list of some of the more prominent ones, see *Literary Market Place*. To learn if there is a writers' guild in your area, contact the education council or the Chamber of Commerce in your city, or watch the newspaper for a calendar of events as these will frequently alert you to this type of organization.

You have now learned about the business of writing. With either a pen, or today the word processor, you know that writing is an art form requiring discipline and perseverance. Writing and your writing talent can now be organized into a business. Read and follow these proven paths to success. They have worked for many writers, and they will work for you too.

PUBLICATIONS OF VALUE TO WRITERS

The following list contains directories and periodicals of value to writers. Some are inexpensive and will be used so frequently that they should be a part of your personal library. Many of these publications can be found in your local library, although reference books usually cannot be checked out for home use. However, some reference directories, such as *Books in Print*, are available on CD-ROM, making the information as close as your fingertips. Most of these directories are updated annually because the information in them quickly becomes obsolete, so be sure to use the most recent edition. For a more extensive list of directories, refer to "Catalogs" and "Publishers" in *Books in Print*. Also, by using the SUBJECT GUIDE of *Books in*

Print you can locate publishers of specific topics, genre, and so forth.

DIRECTORIES LISTING MARKETS FOR BOOKS, ARTICLES, SHORT FICTION, AND POETRY

Literary Market Place, R.R. Bowker, 121 Chanlon Rd., New Providence, NJ 07974. Usually called *LMP,* this publication is especially helpful in locating publishers of books, and includes over 3000 book publisher listings. Also included is a section on book clubs, literary agents, literary contests, and many other subjects related to the publication of books. It also includes a modest listing of magazines that use free-lance material. Also see *International Literary Market Place,* R.R. Bowker, for foreign markets.

Writer's Market, Writer's Digest Books, 1507 Dana Ave., Cincinnati, OH 45207. *Writer's Market* is the marketing directory used most widely by free-lance writers. It includes lists of BOTH book and magazine publishers. It is comprehensive, relatively inexpensive, and contains over 4000 markets.

Novel and Short Story Market, Writer's Digest Books, 1507 Dana Ave., Cincinnati, OH 45207. Market listings are divided into four parts: Literary Magazines, Commercial Periodicals, Small Presses, and Commercial Publishers.

This directory is indexed both by alphabet and category, and each entry includes the editor's name, the kind of fiction published, advice and comments, and payment policies. This reference also contains a list of contests and awards for fiction writers.

International Directory of Little Magazines and Small Presses, Dustbooks, P.O. Box 100, Paradise, CA 95677. This publication includes a comprehensive list of over 5000 markets including literary magazines and small presses. The listings include descriptions of the kind of material each press or magazine publishes, average payment, and editors' names and addresses. The entries are cross-referenced by subject, state, and country.

The Children's Media Marketplace, Gaylord Professionals Publications, 100 Varick Street, New York, NY 10013. This directory lists periodicals, book clubs, television and radio stations looking for youth-oriented material.

Book Publishing Career Directory: Guide to the Top U.S. and Canadian Book Publishers, Career Press Inc., 180 Fifth Ave., Hawthorne, NJ 07507.

Directory of Poetry Publishers, Dustbooks, Box 100, Paradise, CA 95967.

Gale Directory of Publications and Broadcast Media, Gale Research, 835 Penobscot Bldg., Detroit, MI 48226-

4094. Includes lists of magazines, newspapers, radio and television stations located throughout the country.

Ulrich's International Periodicals Directory, (3 volumes), R.R. Bowker, 121 Chanlan Rd., New Providence, NJ 07974.

The Guide to Newspaper Syndication, Suite 326, P.O. Box 19654, Irvine, CA 92720. A tool to help you find the best syndicate for your cartoon or text feature.

DIRECTORIES LISTING MARKETS FOR MOVIE AND TELEVISION SCRIPTS

Pacific Coast Studio Directory, 6331 Hollywood Boulevard, Hollywood, CA 90028.

Scriptwriter's Marketplace, 6715 Sunset Boulevard, Hollywood, CA 90028.

DIRECTORIES LISTING LITERARY AGENTS

Guide to Literary Agents and Art/Photo Reps, Writer's Digest Books, 1507 Dana Ave., Cincinnati, OH 45207.

Literary Market Place, R.R. Bowker, 121 Chanlan Rd., New Providence, NJ 07974.

Literary Agents: A Writer's Guide, Poets and Writers, Inc., 72 Spring St., New York, NY 10012.

The Writer's Handbook, Macmillan, 45 Islington Park St., London, England NI IQB.

Literary Agents of North America, Author Aid, 340 E. 52nd Street, New York, NY 10022.

TRADE MAGAZINES

The following periodicals contain valuable information you can use as you prepare your marketing strategy. They will allow you to keep track of editors as they move to different publishing houses, target successful agents and learn what kinds of material they are seeking, and discover which publishing houses are expanding and which are reducing their lists. They also contain current marketing tips including the types of material specific magazines are needing. While this is important information, it takes considerable time to keep up on the latest word in the publishing world, and you may find yourself torn between reading about where to publish a manuscript and finding the time to write it. This is a conflict that will always tug at you as you strive to become a professional writer.

Byline, P. O. Box 130596, Edmond, OK 73013. A monthly for writers and poets.

Children's Writer, 95 Long Ridge Rd., West Redding, CT 06896. A monthly with valuable tips about manuscripts for children's markets.

Folio, 6 River Bend, P. O. Box 4949, Stamford, CT 06907. A monthly covering the magazine publishing industry.

Freelance Writer's Report, Cassell Communications, Inc., P.O. Box 9844, Fort Lauderdale, FL 33310. A monthly newsletter covering marketing tips and news in both the periodical and book market.

Magazine Week, 432 Park Ave., New York, NY 10016. A weekly covering the magazine publishing industry.

Poets and Writers, 72 Spring St., New York, NY 10012. A monthly magazine for literary writers and poets.

Publisher's Weekly, 205 W. 42nd St., New York, NY 10017. A weekly trade magazine, available by subscription, directed to publishers, writers, and agents. It contains reviews of forthcoming books, trade news, and trends in publishing.

Small Press Review, Box 100, Paradise, CA 95967. A monthly newsletter about small publishers.

The Writer, 120 Boylston St., Boston, MA 02116. A monthly available in bookstores or by subscription. This periodical covers practical articles for writers on how to write for publication and how to market manuscripts.

Writer's Digest, 1507 Dana Ave., Cincinnati, OH 45207. A monthly about writing and publishing. This publication is filled with how-to articles—how to write and sell your manuscripts.

Writer's Journal, 27 Empire Dr., St. Paul, MN 55103. A monthly that covers all aspects of the writing/publishing business.

PROOFREADERS' MARKS

Proofreaders' Marks are used to indicate changes in a manuscript:

Instruction	Mark in Margin	Mark in Type	Corrected Type
Delete	*e*	the ~~ripe~~ apple	the apple
Insert material	*ripe*	the ⅄apple	the ripe apple
Let it stand	*stet*	the ~~ripe~~ apple	the ripe apple
Capitalize	*cap*	the apple	the Apple
Make lower case	*lc*	The apple	the apple
Set in italics	*ital*	How good	How *good*
Set in roman type	*rom*	How *good*	How good
Set in boldface	*bf*	How good	How **good**
Set in light face	*lf*	How **good**	How good
Transpose	*tr*	The apple good	The good apple
Close up space	⊃	The ap ple	The apple
Delete and close	*e*	The appple	The apple

Spell out	(sp)	②apples	two apples
Insert			
space	#	the⁄apple	the apple
period	⊙	This is an apple.	This is an apple.
comma	⌃	apple⌄apple	apple, apple
hyphen	=	apple⌄lemon pie	apple-lemon pie
colon	(:)	The following recipe	The following recipe.
semicolon	⌃;	Wash first⌄ then eat.	Wash first; then eat.
apostrophe	⌄	Tom⌄s apple	Tom's apple
quotation marks	⌄⌄/⌄⌄	Who wants this apple?	"Who wants this apple?"
en dash	$\frac{1}{N}$	1914⌄1918	1914–1918
em dash	$\frac{1}{M}$	The apple⌄how good it is⌄is good for you.	The apple—how good it is—is good for you.
superscript type	⌄2	$2^{\vee} = 4$	$2^2 = 4$
subscript type	⌃2	H⌄O	H_2O
asterisk	*	apple⌄	apple*

Start paragraph	¶	"Where is it?" "It's here."	"Where is it?" "It's here."
Move left		the apple	the apple
Move right		the apple	the apple
Align		the apple the apple the apple	the apple the apple the apple
Wrong font	*wf*	the apple	the apple

GLOSSARY

The following glossary includes words commonly used in the writing business.

Advance: Money a publisher pays to an author after a book contract is signed but before the book is published. The advance is deducted from royalty payments earned from the sale of the book.

All rights: When all rights to a manuscript are sold, the author relinquishes the right to use or sell the manuscript again. The buyer is the owner of the manuscript and can use it once or in many publications without further payment to the author. Many magazines will only print articles if they can purchase all rights. This ensures the material will not appear elsewhere. See page 120 for a discussion of other rights.

Assignment: An editor contracts with a writer to produce a specific manuscript for an agreed-upon fee.

Auction or book auction: When several publishers are interested in purchasing the rights to a book manuscript, bids are offered. The author or agent usually selects the publisher that offers the best "deal," which includes the royalty offered, the amount of advance, promotional budget, size of first printing, etc. This method is also used when selling rights to a book to be used for a movie or television adaptation or printed in paperback form.

B/W or b/w: Abbreviations for black and white photographs.

Backlist: Books on a publisher's list of books in print that are not the publisher's most recent books.

Book packager: Sometimes called a book producer or developer, this individual brings together the talents needed to produce a manuscript including writers, artists, research assistants, and maybe a promoter to develop a marketing strategy. They may also find a publisher.

Byline: Author's name appearing with a published piece.

Caption: A heading to accompany a photograph or an illustration. When preparing a manuscript, these are listed on a separate page, with numbers corresponding to numbers on the photos and illustrations, and placed at the end of the manuscript. A notation is made within the text indicating where each caption and illustration should be inserted.

Circulation (circ.): The number of copies of a publication that are sent to bookstores or purchased by subscription.

Clean copy: A neat, typewritten manuscript, free of errors, cross-outs, and insertions.

Commissioned: A specific article or book written at an editor's request for a price to be paid upon completion.

Contributor's copies: Copies of magazine sent to the author in which the author's work appears. These are used as a source of "tear sheets" to submit to editors as evidence of published work.

Copy-editing: Editing a manuscript for grammar, punctuation, and printing errors, but not subject matter.

Copyright: A legal method used to protect an author's work to prevent copying without permission or compensation.

Cover letter: A brief letter that accompanies a submission to an editor, whether it is an article or a book manuscript, stating what is enclosed.

Feature: A lead or main article in a magazine, usually providing information rather than entertainment.

Filler: A short piece such as a joke, interesting fact, puzzle, or news item that is used by editors to fill empty areas left after the main articles are in place.

Galleys: Manuscript set in type but not always divided into pages. Galley sheets are proofread, and corrections are made before the material is printed.

Genre: Pronounced "jahnrah,"refers to a general classification of writing with categories such as nonfiction or fiction, or to categories within the classification such as romance novels, adventure novels, or science fiction.

Ghostwriter: A writer who is hired to write a manuscript based on information supplied by another person. The other person's name appears as the author.

Glossy: Black and white photos with a shiny surface. This is usually the finish required by publishers.

Illustrations: Anything used to bring visual relief to an article or book including photographs, maps, cartoons, and other artwork.

Imprint: Specific categories of books published by a parent company. Some publishing companies have many imprints (e.g., Simon and Schuster imprints Prentice Hall, Arco, Pocket Books, and others).

IRC: The abbreviation for International Reply Coupon, used for reply mail from foreign markets. These can be purchased at your local post office.

Kill fee: The fee paid when an article was assigned but was not accepted upon completion. This may be due to a change in editorial needs or the manuscript may not meet the quality standards required by the publication. This usually ranges from 1/5 to 1/2 of the fee offered for the article.

Lead time: The amount of time prior to publication that the articles for a magazine are assembled.

Libel: A false statement that might expose another person to criticism or ridicule.

Little magazines: Magazines with small printings and limited circulation. They usually print literary, poetry, and political articles.

Mass market: Books of wide appeal, usually small paperbacks containing romance or adventure.

Midlist: Those books on a publisher's list that are not expected to be big sellers, but have limited, yet steady sales. They are usually written by new or unestablished writers or by established writers on subjects of limited interest.

Model release: This is usually a one-sentence, signed statement that gives permission for a photograph to be published. Some publications require a model release; others do not.

Ms: The abbreviation for manuscript.

Mss: The abbreviation for manuscripts.

Net receipts: The money a publisher receives from the sale of a book after bookstore discounts, sale discounts, and returned books are deducted from gross receipts.

On spec: Stands for "on speculation." An editor agrees to look at a piece for possible publication but is under no obligation to purchase or publish it.

Over-the-transom: Unsolicited books or articles submitted to publishing houses by free-lance writers.

Package sale: A manuscript and accompanying photos and illustrations are purchased by an editor or publisher as a unit. No extra pay is offered for the photos or illustrations.

Page rate: Payment for an article based on the number of published pages it covers rather than on the number of words it contains.

Payment on acceptance: A publisher pays for an article as soon as it is accepted for publication. This is the preferred method of payment.

Payment on publication: A publisher pays for an article after it has been published. This can be many months after it was accepted for publication, and, with no money at risk, the publisher may lose interest and not print the material.

Pen name: A fictitious name used by an author who wishes to remain anonymous.

Photo feature: A feature article that emphasizes photographs with accompanying comments rather than text.

Photocopied submissions: Copies of an original manuscript. Some editors will accept photocopied submissions although they should be informed if copies have been sent to other editors (simultaneous submissions).

Plagiarism: Using another writer's work as your own.

Proofreading: Reading a manuscript for typographical, punctuation, and printing errors.

Proposal: A proposal for nonfiction includes an outline, sample text (one or two chapters), market analysis, and supporting material, sent, along with a query letter, to a publisher or agent in an effort to solicit interest in a project. A fiction proposal should include a letter, synopsis, and at least three chapters of text.

Public domain: Material whose copyright has expired.

Publication not copyrighted: A periodical that is not protected by copyright. After an article has appeared in such a periodical, it cannot be copyrighted.

Query letter: A letter directed to an editor or agent that explains what you have written or want to write and asking for permission to send a complete proposal (see page 104).

Release: A statement that says you are the owner of a manuscript and that it has not been sold to another publication. Most magazines require a release before publishing an article. This also refers to a model release, in which the person(s) in a photograph signs an agreement that the photo can be used for publication.

Remainders: Books that are slow to sell and are sold at a reduced price. An author may not receive royalties on books that are remaindered.

Reporting time: The time period during which an editor or agent will respond to your query or manuscript.

Rights: The privilege to print a manuscript. See Chapter 7 for a discussion of the many types of rights.

Royalties: Money paid by publishers to authors for the use of their work. The royalties for a standard hardcover book are around 10% of the net price for the first 5000 copies sold, 12.5% on the next 5000, and 15% on the remaining books sold. Royalties paid on trade paperbacks are generally around 6% of the retail price on the first 20,000 copies sold, and 7.5% on the copies sold thereafter. The royalties on mass paperbacks range from 4% to 8% of the net price. Royalties paid by a publisher are negotiable.

SAE: The abbreviation for self-addressed envelope.

SASE: The abbreviation for self-addressed stamped envelope. An SASE should be sent with a communication if you ask for a reply or want material returned.

Self-publishing: The author pays for and manages the production of a book, from editing and layout to finding a printer. The author also markets the book and receives all of the income derived from selling it (see page 190).

Sidebar: A chart, list, or other supporting information that elaborates on the text it accompanies. A sidebar is usually enclosed in a box or set apart from the main text in some manner.

Simultaneous submissions: Sending the same article or proposal to several editors or publishers at the same time. The editor should be informed that the work has been submitted elsewhere and the author should withdraw it from consideration after it has been sold.

Slide: A 35mm transparency photograph in a 2" x 2" cardboard or plastic mount. Most editors prefer 35mm slides for color because they reproduce better than color prints.

Slush pile: Unsolicited manuscripts that overflow editorial desks and are looked at only after more urgent or solicited manuscripts have been read.

Speculation: Same as "on spec." An editor will look at a piece but is under no obligation to purchase it for publication.

Subsidiary rights: Rights that can be sold with a book contract or sold separately. These include movie, foreign publication, paperback editions, and other rights.

Subsidy publisher: A publisher produces a book, but the cost of production is borne, all or in part, by the author.

Synopsis: A summary of a book or article that is limited to a single page and used as a part of a proposal or query.

Tear sheet: A sheet from a publication that shows your printed work. Often used to solicit more work.

Trade Books: Books written for the general population, called the consumer market, rather than for professionals. These books are divided into categories such as juveniles, fiction (mystery, science fiction and fantasy, romances, general fiction), and nonfiction (art, cookbooks, travel, nature and gardening, sports and recreation, humor, biography and autobiography, history, and other nonfiction).

Transparencies: Photographic slides instead of prints.

Unsolicited manuscript: A manuscript sent to editors or agents without their prior permission.

Vanity publisher: A publisher who produces a book for a fee and does not pay the author royalties. Also called subsidy publisher (see page 194).

Word processor: A computer program that enables writers to produce text through automated typing, text-editing, and storage.

YA: The abbreviation for "young adult books."

INDEX

278